BEHOLD
THE
RADIANCE
(SELECTED ESSAYS)

By

HILARION M. HENARES, JR.

MANILA
PHILIPPINES
1966

OTHER PUBLICATIONS AND WRITINGS BY HILARION M. HENARES, JR.

WITH FERVOR BURNING — Book of Selected Essays — 1965

WAYS AND MEANS column, The Manila Times

ANG NAGKABALHIN NGA DAGWAY SA ATONG YUTA — regular feature in Bisaya Magazine

DAYTOY AGLUPLUPOS A PAGILIANTAYO — regular feature in Bannawag Magazine

ANG PAGPANIBAG-O SANG ATONG PUNGSOD — regular feature in Hiligaynon Magazine

ANG ATING NAGBABAGONG BANSA — regular feature in Liwayway Magazine

WHITHER INDUSTRY — 1963

OUR ECONOMIC HERITAGE, THE DREAM OF ISAGANI — 1962

PAN MALAYAN COMMON MARKET — PRELUDE TO GREATNESS — 1961

THE PROPOSED TREATY WITH JAPAN — 1961

DECONTROL AND THE CHALLENGE OF CHANGE — 1960

TRAVELS OF AN EISENHOWER FELLOW — 1960

THE GLORY HOUR WILL COME — 1959

A PROPOSAL FOR A PAN-MALAYAN COMMON MARKET — 1958

WITHOUT FEAR OF TOMORROW — 1956

RECTO — 1957

CLASS — 1957
REPORT ON THE RISE OF THE INDUSTRIAL MIDDLE-

Printed by PHILIPPINE TEXTBOOK PUBLISHERS

DEDICATION

TO PRESIDENT DIOSDADO MACAPAGAL — in fond recollection of his changing the Independence Day from July 4th to June 12th, of the Maphilindo days, of that "towering instant when he made our nation stand on the threshold of greatness as a potential leader in Southeast Asia";

TO PRESIDENT FERDINAND MARCOS — in breathless anticipation of an era of true greatness for our nation, free and sovereign at last, imbued with a sense of nationalism and a sense of common destiny;

And to my countrymen with a sincere exhortation to respond to our leaders' "call to greatness", in the same way the English responded to Churchill's words in England's darkest and finest hour:

"Come then, let us to the task, to the toil, to the battle . . . each to his part, each to his station, let us go forward together in all parts of the land. There is not a week, nor a day, nor a moment to be lost".

Come, let us begin.

HILARION M. HENARES, JR.
January 1966

ACKNOWLEDGEMENT

To the Manila Times in which some of these articles have originally appeared in its *Ways and Means* column. And to Susie Detera, Rex De Garcia Lores and Miguel M. Villanueva who arduously pored over the proofs and saw this book through the press.

FOREWORD

The function of a foreword is to introduce a book, and often, too, its author. The function of this particular foreword is simplified by the circumstance that it is possible to speak about the present work and its author at one and the same time.

The author probably needs no introduction to most of us, who try to be familiar with the contemporary Philippine scene. Mr. Henares is well-known in business, economic and political circles not only for his executive enterprise but, more significantly, for his earnestly and honestly expressed views on Nationalism. Because of these views, Mr. Henares is not uncontroversial. But above whatever controversy may turn around his figure, the fact remains that he has held many high and responsible positions in business, education and government, that he has reached far and done much. Done much, too, it must be said, for his country which so desperately needs at the present stage of its economic development, that breed of men who, in Mr. Henares' own words, will not "pay the price of subjection in order to develop."

This in fact is what the present work is about — a collection of Mr. Henares' writings over the last few years on *why* and *how* "we need not succumb in order to grow ... we need not pay the price of subjection in order to develop." It seems a shame that even today Filipino voices can still be heard insisting that the price of growth is surrender, the price of development, subjection, that the Filipino is unable or unwilling to tighten his belt in that time of austerity which all young nations must go through before attaining a sovereign, self-respecting and wholesome maturity.

v

If **Behold the Radiance** helps us to understand why the alternative to Filipino economic nationalism is surrender today and the likely forfeiture of our birthright tomorrow, it will have done very much indeed for all of us. To the extent that it does, we shall all be indebted to the young nationalist, Hilarion M. Henares, Jr.

15 Dec. 1965

Senator LORENZO M. TAÑADA
Republic of the Philippines

CITATION

KNOW ALL MEN BY THESE PRESENTS:

Araneta University hereby honors

HILARION M. HENARES, JR.

For outstanding contribution to the national welfare as an educator, entrepreneur, writer, civic leader, economist, devoted public servant, and a nationalist.

As an educator, and first Dean of the Graduate School of Management Engineering of Feati University, he is responsible for organizing the course and bringing into the country the modern concept of motion study in factory operations, other concepts of scientific business management, and for training students in what was at that time a new line in advance engineering education, and giving the country successful business engineering executives.

As an entrepreneur, he has contributed with his distinguished father in the establishment of an integrated paint industry and of a complex of manufacturing enterprises engaged in the production of chemicals and school supplies. By the managerial ability which he has contributed to these enterprises, he has brought into operation business management of the highest order, which has served as an inspiration for others to follow.

As writer and civic leader, he has contributed to the idealization of the cause of Filipino entrepreneurship, provoked national thinking on issues which today "agitate the national spirit", and given substantive direction to economic thinking in this country.

As economist and public servant, in his capability as Chairman of the National Economic Council, he has institutionalized the rapport and continuing dialogue between private business and government as a necessary condition to the formulation of public policies, and steered the highest economic agency of government into the formulation of economic policies which would place the Filipino in a dominant position over his country's economic affairs.

As a nationalist, Chairman Henares has infused nationalism into government policies, and has given to the Filipino entrepreneur a philosophy and direction which relates his mundane endeavors to the highest interest of his country, of his government, and of his people.

Therefore, Araneta University, upon recommendation of its Academic Council, hereby confers upon Hilarion M. Henares, Jr. this 15th day of May, nineteen hundred and sixty-five, A.D., the degree of Doctor of Economics, Honoris Causa.

SALVADOR ARANETA
President

CONTENTS

PART I — OF MANY THINGS

PART II — ON ECONOMICS

PART I

OF MANY THINGS

In the manner of the celebrated dramatist, Eugene Ionesco, Henares does not stop asking questions, a supreme quality which is characteristic of an engaging and living mind. And in the questions he asks, we are able to perceive the glimmer of the significance of the human effort in our own society and time.

CARLOS P. ROMULO

THE STORY OF MANKIND

The proper study of man is Man. Tell me the story of mankind, begged the sweet young lady with all the curious wisdom of her six years of age. Who can resist the challenge of one on whom the future of mankind depends? Sit still, my child, and listen to fifty million years of human drama, the denouement of which may yet be in your hands.

*   *   *   *   *

Once upon a time, millions and millions of years ago, a strange curious-minded creature stared through matted hair at the brilliant pin-points of light set in the velvety blackness of the night.

He asked himself "Why?" And with that question he drifted away from the beasts of the field and unconsciously started on the road to destiny.

It was a road beset with perils and pitfalls that this bewildered creature took — this half human creature struggling to be a Man.

He was weak, but he was not helpless. His skin was bared to the elements, but he tamed fire to give him warmth and comfort. His was not the agility of the tiger nor the strength of the elephant, but he chipped the sides of a stone to fashion a weapon that gave him mastery over the animal world.

He viewed the fishes roving the deep and found that by gouging out a log into a crude canoe, he too could roam the seas. He watched birds rise in the air and wondered if he too could fly.

Man's progress was slow, and the sun did not always shine on his path.

Once, amidst the terror-laden blackness of the night, he stopped and realized that he was terribly alone. There,

3

in his loneliness, he found a Friend. For out of the night came a voice saying, "I am the Lord thy God . . ."

In a vision of another world, Man saw things more beautiful than he ever saw before. He saw pearly gates and golden streets and jeweled palaces. In seeing, he found peace and contentment and a promise of things to come.

When the vision faded, Man was filled with envious yearning. He could not wait for another world. He wanted his heaven here on earth. He would build it himself, aye, and be like . . . God!

Eagerly, passionately, he set himself upon his task. He took the green of the pastures, the gold of the hills, the might of the rivers, fashioned them with his hands, his heart, his mind — and transformed them into power. He built ships that plowed the heaving oceans, planes that swept the virgin heights.

He bored tunnels through insurmountable barriers of rock. He moved mountains. He sent his merest whisper echoing throughout the world. He conquered time and space, he conquered his whole planet . . .

But he could not conquer himself. Evil crept into his soul and manifested itself in wars, cruelty and bloodshed. He sought peace but he brought only turmoil and confusion unto himself.

A strange restlessness grew within him. The light of knowledge served only to extend the circumference of the surrounding darkness. The more he learned, the more he realized how ignorant he really was, and how utterly unworthy he was of the heaven he was to build.

He who wished to be God found out that he was just a small, crawling mass of impure carbohydrate, marooned in a bit of stardust adrift in the vastness of the infinite.

Then suddenly Man made two tremendous discoveries. In an infinitely minute particle of matter he found the source of the power of suns and stars. Then he discovered the means to free himself from Mother Earth and reach out into the timeless space beyond. The mystery of all creation awaits his coming.

Awestruck and confused, Man stands at the threshold of a new era. The key is in his hand. Hopeful yet afraid, he hesitates at the door before him. What thoughts, what prayers, what visions take place within him!

Perhaps Man can now be a God. Perhaps he can now build his pearly gates and golden streets and jeweled palaces. Perhaps.

But in the light of his human failings, he wonders if he can trust himself with that awesome secret. Perhaps, he was never meant to be a God. Perhaps the revelation of that secret will destroy Man, will blast the world back into its elements . . .

. . . and perhaps, millions and millions of years will pass, before there is a new world and a new planet . . . and another curious-minded creature, staring through matted hair at the brilliant pinpoints of light set in the velvety blackness of the night.

————o————

THE COUNTRY OF THE BLIND

It is said that "in the country of the blind, the one-eyed man is king." This is seldom true. In almost all times and climes, the people blindly resistant to change, have jailed, persecuted, vilified, ostracized, mocked, burned, hanged or shot most any man of vision in a vain attempt to drag him down to the level of their own blindness. This was true of Christ, Galileo, Gandhi, Lincoln, Rizal and many others. This is also true of Claro M. Recto whose birthday we celebrate today (February 8, 1965).

No, I shall not write of Recto's life and works, nor render judgment on him. It would be presumptuous of me or any living Filipino to pass judgment on such a man. What we must fear is the judgment of posterity upon us — his contemporaries and his successors. For this generation of Filipinos will be measured by the ideals and aspirations of this great man.

I offer instead a parable, entitled "The Country of the Blind" from a home movie production starring five-year-old Nena Cabarrus and Ronnie Henares, suggested by a story by H. G. Wells, written and filmed by yours truly in sound and color way back in 1956 at the height of the campaign of vilification against Recto.

*   *   *   *   *

In some far flung outpost of this earth, beyond ranges and ranges of impassable mountains, nestling behind a narrow, forbidding mountain pass which was its only link with the outside world, there was once a country called Sta. Barbara.

One fateful day, a terrible earthquake changed the course of its history. Many, many people died. But the worst was yet to come. The mountains crumbled over the mountain pass, sealing Sta. Barbara off forever from the rest of the world.

6

Then a strange sickness descended upon the hapless people of Sta. Barbara, a sickness that left them completely blind. The sickness grew to epidemic proportions, striking blind every man, woman and child — and soon, even the babies were born blind. And for all succeeding generations, Sta. Barbara became the country of the blind.

Four hundred years passed since that tragic day. Twenty generations came and went. And the people of Sta. Barbara, shut off from the outside world, born blind and living their entire lives in darkness, never knew what it was to see. They developed their sense of touch, their sense of hearing, their sense of smell — and lived normal lives. But the memory of the gift of sight was lost in the obscure mists of the legendary past.

Into this country of the blind, via an airplane crash, came one day a stranger from the outside world whose name was Ronnie.

Ronnie was shocked to find all the people blind and unaware of their blindness. He was even more shocked to find that they regarded him with suspicion because he had eyes to see. The initial suspicion developed into ostracism and derision; and finally into guarded sympathy for the man who was sick and insane because he spoke of stars and moonlight and sunsets which they can neither see nor understand.

Ronnie fell in love with a blind girl named Nena, who also fell in love with him. And together they went to her father and asked his blessing on their love.

Nena's father was a kind, understanding elder but quite adamant about his refusal to give Nena away in marriage to Ronnie . . . unless Ronnie first submitted himself to an operation. Ronnie's eyes were the "irritant bodies causing his madness" and must be rooted out like a cancerous growth.

"You blind fools!" Ronnie cried, "I'll show you that in the country of the blind, the man with eyes is king!"

7

The people laughed at him. He fought them back. Fight the blind? Their senses of smell and hearing were so acute, their sense of direction so set by centuries of habit, that the pople of Sta. Barbara had no difficulty frustrating any attempt to mischief on his part.

"Let's leave him alone," they said, "Poor man, he is sick, sick in the mind, because of those eyes which cause his madness." And everyone left. All except Nena.

Ronnie was ostracized and laughed at because he had eyes to see. It seemed to him, in moments of quiet desperation, that even Nena avoided him — "Oh God! You gave me my eyes to see the redness of the rose and the sunset and all the beauties of this earth. Yet what is the use of having eyes if I can't have Nena? God forgive me, I must submit to an operation! I must!"

And Ronnie submitted himself to an operation. The coals burned red hot in preparation for the operation that was to take out his eyes, the seat of his madness. Slowly he felt the fire coming closer and closer — and suddenly the terrifying moment froze into eternity.

The blazing fire blurred into the flaming red of the roses and the sunset — "No!" Ronnie cried, "No! Let me go!" And he ran away.

Nena called out to him, "Wait, Ronnie, wait! We are only trying to cure your madness."

Ronnie answered, "You do not understand. You cannot understand. I cannot give up something God in his wisdom gave me, even for the love of you. I do not belong here, Nena. I cannot stay here any longer."

And he left. He left Nena sobbing on the ground.

Then he directed himself away from the country of the blind toward the far horizons beyond the ranges and ranges of towering impassable mountains, where he was going away forever.

Scaling precipitous cliffs, upward and onward Ronnie went. Suddenly there was beauty everywhere — a wondrous, breathtaking, awe-inspiring beauty such as no poet can describe . . . grand canyons that bared timeless pages out of nature's book, layer upon layer, singing the saga of milleniums past when earth was young and man was naught . . . illustrating it with pink castles and cathedrals, towers and spires, sculptured by sand, wind and water . . . with shifting kaleidoscopic colors of desert sands as far as the eyes can see . . . with yawning abysmic chasms that stagger the mind into thoughts of time, space, eternity and God!

And Ronnie prayed, "Dear God, let me return some day to this country of the blind. Let me come back with doctors and medicines to cure them of their affliction. Let me bring light to eyes that were meant to see the beauty and wonder of Thy creation!"

But who can divine the mysteries of God's grand design? A slip of the foot and Ronnie fell. Mother Earth miles below opened her arms to receive his broken, bleeding, lifeless body.

And so he died — and with him died all the saints, heroes, martyrs, geniuses, and prophets of this world, who could see farther than most men can.

THE PATRIOTISM OF HUMANITY

A Peace Corps volunteer came to us one day to unburden an uncomfortable thought: "We of the Peace Corps have been college-educated in the finest tradition of American liberalism. We pride ourselves on being internationalists — yet we discover a keen sense of kinship and sympathy with Filipino nationalists."

On the other hand, an American trader, who has been in the Philippines too long and who prides himself on being a super-duper American, volunteered this observation: "Filipino nationalists are chauvinistic and xenophobic — budding Hitlers, I'm afraid. You Flips should try to be more international-minded and serve the cause of the free world above selfish national interest."

To minds mass-produced in the mold of L'il Abner, this is indeed a paradox: The American internationalist and the Filipino nationalist are kindred spirits; the American nationalist and the Filipino "internationalist" are strange bedfellows.

To one imbued with a sense of history, this paradox is no paradox at all but an understandable and logical historical development.

Nationalism is a revolutionary movement born in the West. Dutch and English national consciousness generated the courage and daring that destroyed the might of Imperial Spain; then turned inwards to unleash the forces of liberalism and democracy that destroyed the despotism of Dutch and English kings.

By the 19th century, the spirit of nationalism swept over the diverse peoples of Europe, inspiring them into a belief in their own individual uniqueness, their common historical and cultural heritage, and their right to political unity and self-government. The Poles, the Germans, and the Italians, who possessed no fatherland of their own and

10

were fragmented and ruled by princes of foreign extraction, had grown fiercely conscious of their common destiny and right to liberty and unity.

By 1870 after a score of war-ridden years, the forces of nationalism emerged triumphant. The Germans achieved unification at last under Bismarck. The Italians won unity, independence, and a constitutional government through the efforts of Cavour and Garibaldi. France was transformed from an absolute monarchy to an enduring republic. New emotions for national self-determination were unleashed in the Balkans, long a war-booty of powerful neighbors.

Nationalism brought the industrial middle class into power everywhere, and ushered Europe into the only period of real peace it has ever enjoyed in modern times — characterized by great scientific progress, liberalism, and democracy.

Western nationalism, which was at first a liberative force in Europe, degenerated into Western imperialism in Asia and Africa. National pride turned into arrogance, prejudice, and greed. By some cruel logic, the peoples of Asia and Africa were made to pay the cost in tears, agonies, and death so that the Europeans could be cultured, prosperous, and free.

America's Manifest Destiny, the British Empire upon which the sun never set, Kaiser's and Hitler's Reich, Japan's Co-Prosperity Sphere, and Russia's Third Internationale gave the world no real peace during the troubled 20th century.

The white man's excess of nationalism has brought forth the greatest plagues of humanity today — Western and Communist Imperialism, and the self-doubt and colonial mentality of the oppressed peoples of Asia and Africa.

For they go together in mutual contagion: the sadist and the masochist, the tyrant and the slave, the foreign carpetbagger and the local scalawag, Colonel Blimp and Gunga Din, the super-duper American and his little brown

11

brother, the Communist brain-washer and the brain-washed peasant, the white man's nationalism and the colored man's "internationalism" (which is another name for colonial double allegiance).

The arrogance of the strong keeps company with the cloying obeisance of the weak.
On the other hand, the compassion of the strong keeps company with the dignity of the weak.

Indeed, two liberative forces are stemming the tide of imperialism and colonialism: (1) the enlightened internationalism of the strong nations and (2) the revolutionary nationalism of the weak nations.

The internationalists of the West — Wilson, Russell, Roosevelt, Kennedy, the Peace Corps — are the kindred spirits of the nationalists of Asia and Africa — Rizal, Gandhi, Nasser, Quezon, Recto.

If Woodrow Wilson and John Kennedy were born in the Philippines, they probably would have been Filipino nationalists of the highest order, decrying the impositions of Communists, McCarthyists, and carpet-baggers.

If Jose Rizal and Claro M. Recto were born in the United States, they probably would have been American internationalists concerned with civil rights and the self-determination of oppressed peoples.

For both the Filipino nationalist and the American internationalist are intrinsically of humanist and liberal persuasion. They argue the case of the weak against the strong, and would ask the strong nations to renounce all selfish claims in the larger interests of mankind, especially the oppressed, the wretched, and the poor. They would ask the weak nations to assert their own identity and uniqueness in pride and dignity, and take their place as equals among the rest of the nations of the world.

They would call upon both the strong and weak nations to adhere to what Thomas Mann calls the "Patriotism of Humanity" — to underline the idea that human welfare is indivisible, and to demonstrate the greatest Truth of our

12

times — the truth of which poets sing and philosophers dream:

That across all artificial borders of national sovereignties, above the diversity of political and economic systems, beyond all differences in race, culture, and creed — lies, under God, the *common humanity of man.*

It is this truth that makes men brothers.

It is this truth that will set men free.

DR. JEKYLL AND MR. HYDE

The goodlooking and respected Dr. Jekyll who is kind to animals and little girls, driven by scientific curiosity to concoct a witch's brew, takes a swig of the distasteful stuff and staggers, eyeballs popping, hands clutched at his burning throat. His handsome face contorts itself into ugliness, furry hair sprouts on his face, his mouth twists to reveal fangs, his fingers curl up into claws — presto, he is now Mr. Hyde, a sadistic maniac who prowls the streets to commit mayhem on sirens and old maids.

Grandma remembers him as John Barrymore; mother, as Frederic March; and this generation still remembers him as Spencer Tracy. These three great movie stars launched their careers on a vivid portrayal of the dual personality of "Dr. Jekyll and Mr. Hyde" in performances calculated to fill our nights with fantasies and cold sweat.

But the story has a moral. It serves to remind us of the church teaching that we are all a mixture of good and evil, a legacy of our progenitors' Original Sin. The psychologists interpret it as the struggle between the *Ego* and the *Id* — the *Ego*, our conscious self, striving to conform to the dictates of society outside of one's self; the *Id*, our unconscious self, drawing its motivations from a deepseated reservoir of primordial selfishness that lies within every man, knowing no logic, no values, no morality save the need for its own satisfaction.

It is a well-known fact that a man who feels free of the inhibitions of his accustomed society, reacts and responds unpredictably to his subconscious *Id*.

A respectable husband who is faithful to his wife at home and kneels in prayer before angelus bells sweetly pealing, may find himself in a foreign city ogling with abandon at belles sweatily peeling.

14

A society woman whose heart bleeds for the poor and underprivileged spends her waking hours in social work, neglecting her own children and driving them to juvenile delinquency.

A clean-cut, wholesome young man who grew up in a moralistic Puritan society, is thrown into the mass anonymity of an overseas army and turns out to be a PX smuggler and a bird-killer who can't shoot straight.

Nations have a dual personality too. The British who at home would die to defend the sanctity of home, property and person, sallied forth abroad on a rampage of colonial plunder still unequalled in scope in the annals of history. The Mr. Hydes of the British colonial office have obliged the Asians and Africans to pay the cost in tears, agonies and death so that the Dr. Jekylls at home could be cultured, prosperous and free.

Probably the reason America's image is so tarnished in most parts of the world is that Americans abroad do not really represent the best of the American people at home. The Americans in the United States are of liberal middle-of-the-road persuasion — condemning by anti-trust action the monopolistic tendencies of big business, shackling the militaristic elements of the armed forces through firm civilian control, and putting to public shame Dixiecrats of the Klu Klux Klan variety and McCarthyists who employ Communist methods to combat Communism.

Unfortunately the American image abroad is shaped by a small but vocal minority of Goldwaterite outcasts from President Johnson's Great Society — vested interests who, frustrated at home, now venture abroad spreading the gospel of the kind of monopolistic free enterprise that has spawned robber barons and great depressions; Dixiecrats who, unable to find employment in the economically stagnant agricultural society south of the Mason-Dixon line, join the armed forces and government agencies abroad, bringing with them the bigotry, racial prejudice, and McCarthyism of their unlovely land.

Those who are quick to condemn Americans in general are advised to seek the company of Peace Corps volunteers, who to our mind, represent the finest flower of the American people — liberal, tolerant, generous, freedom-loving, and sensitive to the legitimate aspirations of the people whose hospitality they enjoy.

The point of this article is that no one, except God on Judgment Day, has a right to pass final judgment on a nation, a people, or any individual person — for each at any particular instant of time and place is influenced in his actions and actuations, by the eternal push and pull of the forces of good and evil, *Ego* and *Id*, Dr. Jekyll and Mr. Hyde.

Which of these forces will ultimately prevail?

In all ages, man has looked upon himself as the image of God and believed, as an article of faith, in the inevitable triumph of good over evil.

In the movie, Mr. Hyde is killed and passes on to eternity as the good Dr. Jekyll. The erring husband eventually comes home. The social worker turns to her juvenile delinquent with a mother's love and a firm rod. The PX smuggler and bird-killer is thrown upon the tender mercy of the local courts. The British have changed and are still changing, ushering new prideful nations into being. And by the grace of God and a little help from us, the Americans abroad will comport themselves in the great and glorious traditions of Lincoln, Wilson, Roosevelt, and Kennedy.

Ultimately, good will prevail over evil, the *Ego* will suppress the *Id*, Dr. Jekyll will triumph over Mr. Hyde. And such is the eternal optimism of mankind — such is the indomitability of the human spirit — that the human race and its humanity will endure to the end of time.

————0————

DREAMS, VISIONS AND WILD HOPES

There are many of us who see things as they really are, and ask ourselves — Why?

But we must dream of things that never were, and ask ourselves — Why not?

— ROBERT KENNEDY

There's the difference between the merely curious and the boldly adventurous. The curious ask "Why?"; the adventurous ask "Why not?"

Indeed, why not? In all ages, men fought most valiantly for things that never were, for gardens yet to be planted and cities yet to be built, for beautiful women yet to be loved, heavenly kingdoms yet to be won, and new nations yet to be born.

Dreams, visions, and wild hopes are mighty weapons in the hands of those who plunge into undertakings of great change.

Visions of heavenly kingdom inspired religious movements to civilize the savage tribes of Europe and Asia; dreams of plunder and untold riches ushered in the Age of Discoveries and the mighty colonial empires; hopes inspired by an extravagant concept of man's boundless intelligence brought the world to the Age of Reason, the Industrial Revolution, the Scientific Era, and the Atomic Age.

It was an ancient dream that sustained the Jews through two thousand wandering years back to their home in Palestine, there to build a garden nation out of the sands of the desert.

It is the hope of fabulous achievement and world domination that now spurs the great powers into a race to the stars; and "rising expectations" that keep new nations in a state of revolutionary fervor.

17

How can we renovate our own stagnant society and promote the higher destiny of the Filipino people?

Not by driving the people to despair, as most of our writers and politicians are doing; nor by stirring up discontent, as Communist agitators hope to do; nor by infecting our people with fear, hatred, distrust, and self-doubt, as carpetbaggers and McCarthyists are trying to do; nor by submitting ourselves in humility and in humiliation to the guidance and judgment of foreign mentors, as the little brown brothers want us to do.

No, we must, like the prophets of old, kindle and fan an extravagant hope, based on faith in ourselves, if we are to inspire our people to constructive action.

What hopes, what prayers, what visions take place within us?

Is it too much to hope that someday we will outgrow our Oedipus complex towards Mother America, and pursue our own separate destiny as befits a truly sovereign nation?

Why not? At least 75 per cent of our population are of a new generation without an umbilical cord to our colonial past. In 10 years, they will take over the leadership of our new nation.

Is it too much to dream that someday, we shall make our own friends without the white man's intercession, and make our own plans without the white man's patronage?

Why not? In an era of political and economic giants, new aggrupations of small nations are in the making, in spite of the mischief of great powers — the Latin American Common Market, the Arab League, the Afro-Asian bloc, the African Common Market, and soon, sooner than we expect, a Southeast Asian Common Market, including the Philippines, Malaysia, Indonesia, Thailand, and others.

Is it too much to pray that in the future, the Philippines may yet be in a position of world leadership?

Why not? Time has no beginning, no end — only a perpetual unfolding. Nations are born, they grow old, and they will surely die — so it was with the empires of Egypt, Rome, Spain, and America's own Mother Britain — so will it be with Russia, Red China, and our own Mother America in the next Armaggedon. But the Philippines is still undergoing its birth pains, and God willing, it will survive to greatness as the leader of Southeast Asia.

Why not? The Philippines is young, as young as England was at the outset of its Industrial Revolution, as young as the United States was after the Civil War — with 30 million people in an area and with resources that can support 100 million, large enough to provide capacity for industrialization, yet small enough to industrialize without the insurmountable pressures of population growth . . . young enough to surpass someday the age-old history-weary population-laden nations of India, China and Japan.

Why not? Of all Southeast Asian nations, the Philippines is the most literate, the most cultured, the most aggressively entrepreneurial, the most economically advanced, the most industrialized, the most politically mature, the most socially mobile with no traditional class barriers — the only English-speaking country in an area where English has become the universal language — the only Christian country where Christianity represents the most enlightened way of life — the most westernized, the most democratic, the most liberal country where western democratic liberalism represents the most progressive force.

Why not, indeed? When the great land masses are contaminated by atomic radiation, when the Malthusian nightmare of population exceeding the means of production becomes stark reality — Southeast Asia under the leadership of the Philippines stands astride the greatest oceanic continental shelf on earth, where undersea farms and undersea mines can provide food and necessities to a future world bereft of its resources. And the Philippines in its turn may conceivably be a colossus bestride the universe.

Why not? The torch of civilization was passed in one unbroken line from Greece to Rome to Great Britain and Spain to the United States — from mother to son, from colonizer to the colonized — why not then to America's only ward, the Philippines, in a future world no longer willing to accept the leadership of the white minority?

Dreams, visions, and wild hopes!

Why not, indeed?

THE LOST GENERATION?

There is a time in the history of every nation when one generation stands out to proclaim, with a kind of perverse pride, that it is the "lost generation" and the worst in the nation's history.

The generation of Englishmen during the First Industrial Revolution and the generation of Americans after the Civil War were so damned by the testimony of their own living witnesses and intellectuals, as is our own generation of Filipinos today — for frontier lawlessness, shameless exploitation of the masses, the plundering greed of robber barons, the rampant graft and corruption of public officials, moral decay and widespread crime, recurrent financial scandals and crises, economic panics and depressions.

But the witness cannot be a judge. The final judgment on any age must properly belong to the historian from the safe distance of decades hence when all facts and forces, all persons and events may be entered on both sides of the ledger and evaluated with detachment and dispassion.

By the very verdict of history, the two aforementioned generations of Englishmen and Americans, each in its own time and place, did usher their respective nations through their greatest period of growth and set the stage for their emergence as world powers. Notwithstanding their self-flagellation, they were adjudged the best generations their nations ever produced.

How about our present generation of Filipinos?

There is so much to grieve about in our tide of times.

There are the plunderers of our patrimony: those who dynamite our seas, despoil our ancient timber stands and watersheds, disembowel our mineral-laden mountains, exhaust the fertility of our soil, surrender sovereignty and parity rights for a mess of potage — all for benefit of self without any thought of the irretrievable losses to the rest of the nation and to future generations.

There are the corruptors of our citizenry: the smugglers who sabotage our economy by catering to alien-induced appetites; the flesh-peddlers, the dope pushers; politicrats and influence peddlers; policemen and judges so lazy and corrupt that people seem to lose faith in justice and take the law into their own hands; the caciques, the colonial traders and all the economic parasites who fatten themselves on the fruits of another man's labor —

But worst of all, the paid pipers of the modern Carthaginians, who infect our people with fear, hatred, distrust of each other, self-doubt and colonial double-allegiance, singing with insidious sublety a hymn of hate, a dirge of despair, a siren song of damnation, with but one set of lyrics:

"Filipino men sell their souls; Filipino women sell their honor; Filipino businessmen are thieves; Filipino labor and management are no better than Negroes and Red Indians; Filipino political leaders are liars and crooks; Filipino intellectuals and nationalists are communists, — everything Filipino is no good, and therefore Filipinos should resign from the human race and submit themselves in humility and in humiliation to the guidance and judgment of foreign god-men."

Are we indeed the "lost generation"? Perhaps we are lost, in the same way the Americans after the Civil War and the English during the Industrial Revolution were lost — lost in the sense that we were born without an umbilical cord to the colonial past. Perhaps, we are lost in the sense that we are adrift on a sea of watchful uncertainty, waiting for the wave of the future to carry us on to our destiny.

Admit it or not, to use the words of Emmet John Hughes, our generation is caught in the throes of historic change, and the challenges of our time — as they test and torment us who live in it — are varied in size and shape, in meaning and direction, darting in and out in ruthless random.

Some seem black and blunt and staggering, making us reel back and fight for balance — such as the stark realization that foreign carpetbaggers can spin a web of corruption to strangle our economy and government, and that there are many Filipinos whose allegiance is pledged to a country other than the Philippines.

Some seem silvery and swift and wispy as they dart maddeningly past the clutch of outstretched hands — such as the dream that almost came true, to unite all Malayan brothers in the concept of Maphilindo and in a Southeast Asian Common Market.

And yet others loom golden and great and awesome leaving us to do little but turn and gasp as they soar overhead — such as the rise of a great industrial middle class over the faded aristocracy of caciques and colons, making us a modern industrialized democratic nation, at last free and truly sovereign, assuming leadership in our part of the world.

Perhaps, the birth of a nation, like the birth of a baby, is a mixture of pain and joy.

In such a birth, the pain rises sharply till it is almost unbearable, then slowly ebbs away.

And the miracle of birth is such that when the pain passes, only the joy remains.

THE MAN OF THE TWENTIETH CENTURY
(with apologies to Time Magazine)

When Clio, the muse of history, finally closes her diary at the end of the second millenium of the Christian era — whom will she choose as the Man of the 20th Century?

Unless by the year 2000 A.D. there appears a new and extraordinary saint, Clio will have to choose between two ungainly men with unheroic mien — one, a German intellectual with a yen for children and Aeschylus; and the other, an American log-splitter with a penchant for telling funny stories.

At first glance Clio's dates seem wrong. For both men lived and died the century before — the German died peacefully in his easy chair in 1883, the American violently in a theater seat in 1865.

But this is just a technicality, a mere biological accident. In the historic sense, Karl Marx and Abraham Lincoln have just begun to live — and the 20th century is to see them both like two colossi bestride our universe.

This month (February, 1965) marks an anniversary for each — the 117th anniversary of Marx's Communist Manifesto, and the 156th anniversary of Lincoln's birth. Last month marked the 102nd anniversary of Lincoln's Emancipation Proclamation.

"Marxist" is the word that divides the modern world. In the land mass above the Adriatic and the Himalayas all the way to the shores of the Bering and the China Seas, what men consider good is called "Marxist." In the lands both sides of the North Atlantic Ocean, what men consider evil is called "Marxist." In many other parts of the world men are still arguing, fighting and dying over whether the word "Marxist" should mean good or evil.

But everywhere, too, specially where backward peoples are awakening from the dark sleep of centuries into a modern world, it is the name of Abraham Lincoln that is most invoked — against racial prejudice and involuntary servitude, against the intolerable abuses of a landed aristocracy, against the extraneous forces that divide a nation against itself.

Marxism is a fully developed godless religion complete with church, creed and catechism. Its philosophy revolves around The Machine which the Industrial Revolution brought into being — a philosophy that has been proven wrong many times but continue to persist.

That The Machine is pure evil and should be ignored or destroyed is the idea of the fading landed aristocracy and a group of village idiots called Luddites. That The Machine is pure good and would lead to ever greater prosperity is the idea of capitalists. The Marxists took the Machine and made it the center of a class struggle — between capitalists who would "use the powers of the state to limit production, maximize profits and oppress the poor," and the workers who would seize the state by revolution, use its powers to control The Machine, and usher the world into a "classless society of unlimited prosperity."

The Marxist strategy lies in the dialectic method. The usual way of thinking about causes and effects is to imagine them as a chain, one link leading to another link. But the Marxist dialectic moves in a spiral — every idea or "thesis" has its opposite "anti-thesis" with which it struggles until both produce a third idea called "synthesis"; this synthesis in turn has its own anti-thesis with which it must struggle to produce another synthesis.

Marx expressed history by putting class conflicts in the place of thesis and anti-thesis . . . until the last synthesis, which is unique in that it does not have its own self-negation, brings forth the ultimate utopian classless society.

The Marxist imagines history as moving in spiral twists and turns. He sees nothing wrong in allying himself in turn with democratic labor movements, the reactionary landed aristocracy, the Christian Socialists, then with the Nazis, then with the Western imperialists, then with Asian and African nationalists. He is not being cynical or inconsistent. He is being "systematic" in the belief that the struggles between these groups will bring about a series of "syntheses" that will lead to his revolutionary goal in whose inevitability he has blind faith.

The ideas that Lincoln stands for — industrialization, nationalism, humanitarianism, democracy — were not his own. But in his appointed hour, in the crucible that gave birth to his nation, Lincoln became the symbol of all those ideas that now give inspiration and guidance to the many new nations emerging in the world today, including our own country.

In Lincoln's time, the northern United States had just gone through an industrial revolution, an industrial middleclass came into being, asking for higher tariffs to protect its infant industries. The South had still an agricultural economy, under the control of a landed aristocracy using slave labor, selling cotton to Great Britain and demanding free trade to be able to enjoy cheap imported goods. Foreign experts from Great Britain were still lecturing Americans about the law of Comparative Advantage and the folly of protecting local industries.

Encouraged by Britain's moral support and determined to preserve its way of life based on the institution of black slavery, the South seceded. President Lincoln, who was willing to compromise on the preservation but non-extension of slavery, nevertheless went to war to preserve the unity of the nation. "Save the Union!" was his first battlecry; later, as the agricultural South slowly succumbed to the industrial North, the war aim became "Abolish Slavery!"

It was Lincoln's words that revealed the grandeur of his mission:

". . . I hold that if the Almighty had ever made a set of men that should do all the eating and none of the work, He would have made them with mouths only, and no hands; and if He had ever made another class that He intended should do all the work and none of the eating, He would have made them without mouths and all with hands ...

"... A house divided against itself cannot stand ...

"... That this nation, under God shall have a new birth of freedom, and that government of the people, by the people, and for the people, shall not perish from the earth ...

"... With malice towards none, with charity for all, with firmness in the right, as God gives us to see the right, let us strive on to finish the work we are in; to bind up the nation's wounds ... to do all which may achieve and cherish a just and lasting peace, among ourselves and with all nations ..."

For the long suffering races of 20th Century Africa and Asia, Lincoln's spirit lives again — ushering the birth of new nations "conceived in liberty and dedicated to the proposition that all men are created equal."

African diplomats who were a generation away from head-hunting, and who now take their places head erect as equals to the other leaders of the world, have inspired the American Negroes to fight for their own unfulfilled freedoms ... and take their rightful place in Kennedy's New Frontier and Johnson's Great Society. Lincoln's "truth is marching on" and has come to a full circle around the world back to the land of its birth.

Marx and Lincoln have shaped our times and the world we live in — Marx by cold war and class conflicts, to a winter of discontent; Lincoln by the rebirth of old and tested values — industrialism, nationalism, humanitarianism, democracy — to a spring of eternal hope.

———o———

THE GREATEST AMERICAN OF ALL

Did any lover of trees have a daybreak dream
Of a Great Oak on a high hill
Under the flash of a lightning prong
Crashing down helpless —
A loss for all time to the winds and the sky
Who had loved it —
And not known how much they loved it?

— CARL SANDBURG

On Good Friday, April 14, 1865 — exactly 100 years ago today — Abraham Lincoln was assassinated. The assassin, believing that he was ridding his country of a bloody tyrant, echoed the cry of Brutus as he drove the dagger into imperial Caesar: *Sic semper tyrannis!*

But a tree is best measured when it is down. And according to the judgment of eminent historians gathered in Harvard a few years ago, Abraham Lincoln was the greatest of all American presidents.

Second greatest was George Washington; third greatest was Franklin Delano Roosevelt; Truman was among the near-great; Eisenhower, surprisingly, was third from the worst; Kennedy and Johnson at the time were yet to be elected.

A time of great change always cries out for a great leader. It was such a time in the United States when Washington led his people through the birth of a nation. It was such a time when America went through a great depression and almost lost its faith in its politico-economic system, and Roosevelt was called upon to give his people new faith in a New Deal — a Keynesian Capitalism with a social conscience.

But the time of greatest change was that of Abraham Lincoln. It was a time in the United States comparable

28

to our own time in the Philippines today under President Macapagal.

The United States of Lincoln was torn between the Industrial North — "a growing World Power, gigantic in commerce and industry" — and the Agricultural South which had a "King Cotton" colonial economy tied to Mother Britain.

The Philippines also witnessing the rise of a new industrial middle class whose nationalistic aims conflict with those of a landed aristocracy dependent on "King Sugar" exports to Mother America.

One cause of the Civil War was the Northern States' high tariff policy which hurt the South and the British manufacturers. As the British Whig leader, Lord Palmerston, said to Abraham Lincoln: "We do not like slavery, but we need cotton and hate your Morill protective tariff."

Here in the Philippines, our tariff policy designed to protect local industries also came under the attack of the Sugar barons and the American government. At one time the U.S. Commerce Secretary Hodges minced no words lecturing Philippine Ambassador Amelito Mutuc on the need to lower our tariffs.

Lincoln's Emancipation Proclamation which freed the Negroes from slavery is analogous to our Land Reform Code which finally declared illegal the 400-year-old share cropping system that has kept the mass of our tenant farmers in virtual feudal serfdom.

Macapagal's revival of the dream of Malaya Irredenta, as envisioned by Rizal, Quezon and Vinzons, is analogous to the precipitate westward drive of the United States to carve a nation from coast to coast.

Was the great Abraham Lincoln immune to criticism? Not any less than Diosdado Macapagal.

The *New York World* accused Lincoln of trampling on free speech and free press, of "one-man rule," of infrequent cabinet meetings, and decried that the nation was "divided by traitors, ridden by fanatics and cursed with an imbecility in administration only less criminal than treason."

As nationalists berate a nationalistic Macapagal, so did abolitionists berate an abolitionist Lincoln for being "slow and hesitating where vigorous action was required."

Did President Lincoln want to be re-elected? Not any less than Macapagal. A *New York Times* correspondent reported an interview with Lincoln: "He began by saying he was not a candidate for renomination. He distinctly denied that he was a party to any effort to that end." Nevertheless, in spite of opposition from his own party members, Lincoln was renominated and reelected.

The economic situation? Carl Sandburg in his book on Lincoln reports: "Prices of food and clothing soared upward while wages stood still . . . The year 1864 saw more strikes than all the previous years in American history. The national debt reached astronomical proportions, almost bankrupting the government."

Scandals? There was smuggling, prostitution, graft. "A bureau of the Treasury made a house of seduction and prostitution. Members of Congress putting their mistresses into clerkships. Whisky drinking ad libitum. The government cheated in contracts and openly robbed by its employees. Washington was never quite as villainously corrupt . . . at least 20 percent, if not 25 percent of government expenditures were tainted by fraud."

Yet Lincoln in his time broke the back of the Agricultural South, freed the slaves, kept the nation together, and set the stage for America's greatest period of economic growth and emergence as a World Power.

Said *Harper's Weekly* at the time of his death: "Wiser than passion, more faithful than fury, serene in his devotion to the equal rights of men, he tranquilly persisted, enduring the impatience of what seemed to some his *painful delays* and to others his *lawless haste;* and he fulfilled his great task so well that he died more tenderly lamented than any ruler in history."

He died. And the story of the living and actual Lincoln came to an end. Now began the vast and epic tale of the authentic Lincoln tradition mingled with myth and folklore, spreading to all corners of the earth — with one sweeping and beautiful judgment: "He was humanity."

He was the greatest American that ever lived. And he lived in a time of America's history that is analogous to our own time, here and now, in this administration of President Macapagal.

What has history in store for us?

THE CURSE OF SISYPHUS

A curse weighs heavily upon the Filipino nation. It is the curse of Sisyphus.

In Greek mythology, Sisyphus was a Corinthian king who was condemned in hell to roll a big stone up a steep hill. But before it reached the top of the hill, the stone always rolled back downhill and Sisyphus had to start all over again. He was damned for all eternity to seek the summit of fulfillment, only to be mocked again and again by the failure of his hopes.

Such is the hellish curse that blights the progress of our nation since we got back our independence in 1946.

By accident or design, no president of our new born republic was ever yet reelected to serve up to the constitutional limits of a second term.

We had no sustained leadership through the most crucial years of our nationhood. We kept "changing horses in midstream" without realizing the need for continuity of effort in nation-building.

And so we build, only to abandon or destroy, then to start again and build anew. We have become a nation of half-built houses standing amidst the debris of shattered dreams and unfulfilled hopes.

Take the example of our "land for the landless" policy. In Quezon's time just before the war, this policy was implemented by the National Land Settlement Administration (NLSA) under Gen. Paulino Santos; in the Roxas administration, by the Rice and Corn Productivity Administration (Ricpa); in Quirino's time, by the Land Settlement Development Corporation (Lasedeco); in Magsaysay's time, by the National Resettlement and Rehabilitation Administration (NARRA). The succession of agencies and accompanying changes of personnel and work programs conspired to frustrate our great expectations.

Likewise, in almost every sector of the national scene, the curse of Sisyphus was at work. Roads were started, never to be finished, leading nowhere. Railroads, irrigation dams were unfinished, unrepaired. New industries were encouraged only to be abandoned to the mercies of unfair foreign competition, *ad nauseam*.

Every president-elect soon finds out that he assumes office with two strikes against him . The sheer size of the government machinery, with all the old fossils embedded in the civil service, the intricate system of laws, rules, and regulations, the checks and balances — all conspire to thwart any pretensions to sensationally new changes. There are far too many levers to pull, too many switches to flip; the whole machinery simply does not respond to the impatient jab of the finger or the angry pounding of the fist.

He finds that the problems plaguing the nation need solutions with a longer gestation period than just four years — that most of what is happening during his first term of office are the legacies of previous administrations — and that the pitifully little which he can do within his term is to plant the seeds that may bear fruit in some future administration.

By the time the President has learned his job, planned out his course of action, selected the proper men, and made a good start, he realizes that one term is not enough — that a second term of office is necessary to finish the job he started.

And so he reaches out for the magic and elusive "second term" — so far denied to any president since the birth of our republic — to actually finish the work for which he has spent a large part of his first term learning, planning and starting; and to do so without the usual political imperatives that plague a first term of office. But the curse of Sisyphus hangs over his head like the sword of Damocles.

Psychologists say that continued and unbearable frustrations can drive a person into a state of schizophrenia —

33

in which he assuages his disappointments by fantastic self-delusion. Can this also happen to a nation and to a whole people?

Perhaps, we Filipinos have indeed been so mocked by the failure of our hopes that we fall into a frenzy of self-delusion, a drama of self deception, every election time — which is at best an escapist piece of entertainment, at worst an exercise in futility.

The script is always the same, although the cast of characters may change. The electorate says in effect to the candidate for the presidency of the republic:

"Promise us no less than the fulfillment of all our unrealized hopes and unfulfilled dreams — and we shall elect you to office. If we do elect you, you are given four years to perform miracles, to fulfill all our aspirations, four years to start and finish a task which have taken other nations a whole generation to do. If you fail, we shall repudiate you and every little thing you have done so far. And we will elect somebody else to start all over again."

The people do not realize that the failure of our hopes is due, not to the failure of the leader, but to the utter falsity of our hopes.

And so our nation moves, not ever forward, but up and down like the rolling stone of Sisyphus, and will continue to do so unless the Filipino people at last realize that the time must come to take a chance on a magic "second term" and the grand opportunity that it offers: a sustained leadership at last, relatively free from the blight of internecine politics, to inspire our people to transform our nation and renovate our stagnant society beyond the point of no return — to push that damned rolling stone to the summit of fulfillment and free us at last and forever from the hellish curse of Sisyphus.

MACAPAGAL'S SENSE OF HISTORY

We have written much about the need for sustained leadership in times of historic change, as there had been in the time of Manuel L. Quezon ..... as there might have been in these postwar years had Manuel Roxas or Ramon Magsaysay not met untimely death.

We wrote of the pressing need for "a Moses to unite us in common hope for a promised land" as indeed most other nations have had at birth or rebirth — Nasser of Egypt, Ben Gurion of Israel, Nehru of India, Adenauer of Germany, de Gaulle of France and even Chiang of Taiwan.

What are the qualities that make for historic greatness in a national leader?

There had been great leaders, some good, some evil, who walked upon this earth and changed it beyond recall. They have been of different races, of diverse faiths, of divergent personalities — Christ, Caesar, Charlemagne, Napoleon, Ataturk, Aguinaldo, Gandhi, Hitler, Roosevelt, Churchill —but there is one quality they share, and that is a *deep sense of history*.

A sense of history — an appreciation of the past, a faith in the future, and a grand illusion that the present is the time for self-sacrifice and united action in order to link a glorious past with an equally glorious future. The leader must be able to translate this sense of history into a mighty movement for great purposes.

President Macapagal, for instance, showed a remarkable sense of history when he saw himself as part of a continuing but unfinished revolution that started with the "military phase" by which Aguinaldo united our tribal peoples into one nation, then with the "political phase" by which Quezon led us to political independence, and now the "economic phase" by which Macapagal hopes to indus-

35

trialize our nation and set the stage for our emergence as a world power.

He has the dramatic sense of history that inspired him to magnify a trivial fleeting event to serve a distant goal — such as the changing of the Independence Day from July 4 (as decreed by the Americans) to June 12th when we declared our nationhood to the world.

Trivial? There was a time during the early 1950's, when a group of young intellectuals wanted to dramatize the importance of June 12th by publishing a full page advertisement — with a picture of the empty Luneta grandstand and grounds, and the ghosts of our heroes marching by, with the caption: "We march alone on *our* Independence Day." The young intellectuals could not raise the money from businessmen, and they were strongly made to understand that such was an act of utter ingratitude to Mother America, and an unspeakable act of Communist subversion! We had sunk so low in our colonial puppetry that we dared not have even the slightest dint of national pride or loyalty to our own country!

There was a psychological barrier — the same barrier America had to fight two wars with Mother Britain to surmount — there was this mental block that was involved in that "trivial" matter of our independence date. All presidents wanted to do something about it but dared not.

But Macapagal dared to do it. He dared to do the unthinkable, and the shock wave broke the psychological barrier — and then all of a sudden, we were heady with the brew of new-found freedom. From then on, anything was possible.

What subsequently happened?

For the first time since our independence, we dared to pursue an independent foreign policy. Macapagal dared to lay claim to North Borneo long alienated from us by a bunch of British 1-2-3 artists. He dared to revive an ancient dream of Rizal, Quezon and Wenceslao Vinzons — the unity of Malayan brothers through Maphilindo. He

36

had the sense of history to spurn the mean arithmetic of expediency for the act of utter courage — a magnificent gamble that held no hope beyond the audacity of his own imagination. Never before in our colonial past, and probably never again in the foreseeable future, would we Filipinos be more *proud* to be Filipinos, than in that towering instant when Macapagal made our nation stand on the threshold of greatness, as a potential leader among Southeast Asian nations.

But we were not ready because we were not strong. We did not have the strength of will that comes with a sense of *nationalism,* nor the strength of physical power that comes with *industrialization.*

To give us that strength of will, Macapagal actually achieved, without seeming so, what Recto tried to do in his lifetime — kindle a mass revolutionary fervor, a sense of nationhood, a national pride, a national conceit — a creative conceit that makes possible the impossible. Never since the time of Quezon were we Filipinos more nationalistic than we are now, and our nationalism is already irreversible.

To give us that strength of physical power, to pursue the quest for industrialization, Macapagal fathered two events of momentous significance; (a) the Land Reform Code, and (b) the 5-year Socio-Economic program.

To destroy the power of the landed aristocracy that has kept us for centuries in feudal stagnation, Macapagal proceeded to break the 400-year-old socio-economic relationship between the owners of the land and the tillers of it. It was the same historic decision that England made with the "enclosure movement" and the Repeal of the Corn Laws — the same Lincoln made with his Emancipation Proclamation — the same land reform movement that Japan had under Emperor Meiji, and Turkey under Kemal Ataturk.

To usher the mass of our people through the grand adventure of industrialization into an emerging middle class, Macapagal instituted his 5-year Socio-Economic Program. There were many such programs before, but Macapagal was the first President to make it official — and to serve notice that economic development is to be the supreme and over-riding objective of his administration.

But the most significant thing about Macapagal's 5-year Program is that it is *first* of many other programs to follow — a second, then third, etc., 5-year Programs that will give us a sense of continuity of effort in our nation-building. This is the normal procedure for other newly developing nations such as India and Pakistan — so that at each stage, we can measure how far we have gone and how far we have yet to go before reaching the point of self-sustaining growth.

But it is the most immediate and paramount task of a great national leader to ensure a sustained leadership for the nation, to be sure he is around to finish the work he has started. And so, Macapagal must pursue the political imperatives needed to secure that magic, elusive "second term" so far denied, by accident or design, to any of his predecessors.

The months will pass, the days roll by, the hours toll, the minutes tick, inexorably towards that moment when the people of this country — the waving, cursing, cheering millions of the electorate — shall troop, one by one into the voting booth. There quietly and alone — in that instant of sublime solitude when they are so utterly sovereign — they will render their final decision.

Till then, the history of the next four years — and probably of the next hundred years — will stand, waiting, poised and ready — waiting to be suddenly launched and set upon its course.

RIZAL, THE SUBVERSIVE

Today (June 19, 1965) is the 104th anniversary of the birth of Dr. Jose Rizal, *the first Asian nationalist* who in the context of our times has already moved the world.

On the eve of the second conference of the Afro-Asian bloc in Algiers — now that Asian nationalism is a force to be reckoned with, fanning winds of revolutionary change against the redoubts of Western colonialism, Communist imperialism and the ancient scourges of poverty, ignorance and feudal stagnation — perhaps, it may not be amiss for us Filipinos to remind our fellow Asians what we ourselves seldom realize:

That we Filipinos, under the inspiration of Rizal, made the *first nationalist revolution in Asia* in 1896, a revolution that survived up to 1901;

That in 1946, exactly a half century after Rizal's martyrdom, we became the *first people in all of Asia* to achieve independence from Western colonialism.

As most Filipino and Asian nationalists today, Rizal in his own time was called a *filibustero*, a subversive. As a matter of fact, his last novel was difiantly called "El Filibusterismo."

Rizal was a many-sided genius, but he was most of all a writer and a journalist. His brilliant and penetrating satire did more to undermine the intellectual and moral pretensions of Western colonialism than any physical act of rebellion that preceded the Philippine Revolution.

Rizal described himself as a Deputy for the Philippines, in his writings in the *La Solidaridad*, his ear vigilantly cocked for any criticism of the Philippines or the Filipinos, any sneer, any innuendo — ready always to reply, to point out errors, to unmask motives, to expose malice and corruption.

When the Spaniards called Filipinos "ungrateful sons," as a few foreign colons are prone to call today's American-educated nationalistic Filipinos, Rizal replied with all the indignation of today's J. V. Cruz:

"If they take us for ingrates, we will be so bold as to reply to them face to face that if, in exchange for the education they give, they require from us that we forswear the truth and the voice of our conscience — that we stifle the cries of that something God has put within our breasts — and that we suppress our sense of justice in order to sacrifice to their opulent interests, the interests of our native country, our fellowmen and our brothers — then we curse and repudiate their education, and let them never expect from us the least measure of gratitude."

Rizal was the leader of a valiant band of "propagandists' as they called themselves, who were driven to exile, and who wrote in *La Solidaridad*, the nearest thing to a free press at the time. It was a motley group — Marcelo del Pilar who used the pseudonym Plaridel, Mariano Ponce, Lopez Jaena the rabble-rouser, Antonio Luna, Paterno, Lete. As always in any Filipino group, there were the spendthrifts, the gamblers, the womanizers, the compromisarios who sought reforms through humble petitions, and those who preferred to take the offensive openly, defiantly, courageously with intellectual controversy and even physical combat.

There was the hot-headed Antonio Luna who sought out an arrogant Spanish journalist in a cafe, and in his own words, "asked him who he was (I did not know him), called him a vile despicable coward, spat in his face and threw him my card . . . In this way I believe I can show that we Filipinos have more dignity, courage and honor than this cringing and insulting coward who has crossed our path. I think I have satisfied our outraged honor."

The outraged and outrageous Luna might have been reborn in the later day Secretary of Labor Bernardino Abes, who, having overheard to the limit of his patience the loud, arrogant and insulting remarks of an American official against the President in particular and the Filipino

40

people in general, invited the official outside and with consummate skill and appropriate ceremony laid him out horizontally on a bed of flowers.

Rizal was a revolutionary, a subversive who, in a manner that reminds us of President Macapagal calling for his Unfinished Revolution, wrote:

"In order that the Filipino may make progress, it is necessary that a revolutionary spirit should boil in his veins since progress necessarily requires change; it implies the overthrow of the sanctified past by the present, the victory of new ideas over the accepted ones . . . The lack of a national consciousness gives rise to another evil, which is the absence of all opposition to measures prejudicial to the people and the absence of any initiative in whatever may redound to their good."

Rizal might have calling for opposition to today's parity rights, foreign monopoly on drugs, racial discrimination in the bases and in foreign subsidiaries, and the offensive familiarity with which these sacred sows and brazen idols intrude upon centers of political influence.

For their "filibusterismo", Rizal and his band of propagandists suffered, as present-day nationalists and intellectuals are made to suffer, the indignities of the loyalty check, the closed doors of opportunity, the pangs of penury, the whispered lie and secret dossier. In Rizal's time, they suffered more in tears, agonies and death.

Yet Rizal and his valiant band did provoke the aery surge of nationalism that is now sweeping across Asia and Africa, a "wild spirit that is moving everywhere" except so it seems, in the Philippines, the land of its birth.

To recapture that spirit, to catch once again the breath of revolutionary fervor is the task of today's Filipino nationalist. To exclaim in mighty harmony to the winds of Asian nationalism, as the freest of souls, Shelley, once expressed it:

If I were a dead leaf thou mightest bear,
If I were a swift cloud to fly with thee

41

A wave to pant beneath thy power,
And share the impulse of thy strength . . . .
Oh lift me as a wave, a leaf, a cloud!
I fall upon the thorns of life — I bleed . . . .
Be thou, Spirit fierce, my spirit!
Be thou me, impetuous one! . . .
Be through my lips to unawakened earth
The trumpet of a prophecy!

The trumpet of a prophecy — for today's Filipino nationalist knows, as Rizal and his valiant band always knew in their hearts, that if winter comes with all its bitterness and frustration, the spring of fulfillment will not be far behind.

—————O—————

ANTI-FILIPINO CABAL

Not all Americans abroad are ignorant and arrogant. Much good can be said of top US AID officials, priests, some Peace Corps volunteers, and those who are in joint business ventures with Filipinos.

But the recent public outcry about racial discrimination in foreign subsidiaries has focused attention on a different breed of American rarely found in the United States itself. This is the same breed that proliferated in the Philippines during colonial days by the testimonies of no less than Sen. Harry B. Hawes, Gov. Gen. Francis B. Harrison, and Gov. Gen. William Howard Taft who later became the president of the United States.

By special request of our readers, we are reprinting the testimonies of these great Americans, leaving it to the Filipino people to resolve whether or not this peculiar breed still exists in our free and sovereign republic.

"There is a group which has been jokingly called Manila Americans . . . They are prejudicial to the amity that ought to characterize the relations of the American people and the Filipinos. This group is far from friendly . . . Indeed its members provoke racial antagonisms . . . by their disregard or open contempt for the Filipino's pride of race and by their covert attacks on his character and capacity.

"Some of these Manila Americans have acquired property, businesses; others represent American investors or manufacturers. They individually have no very great financial stake in the Philippines, but have constituted themselves, nevertheless, spokesmen for all Americans, and resent on the part of a visitor from States any expression of opinion which has not been first censored by them.

43

"In a way the Manila Americans are dear old boys. Their sense of importance and responsibility as the mentors of Uncle Sam is amazing, and therefore also amusing.

"They have come to believe, I am sure, that they symbolize the might and majesty of the United States. Some of them have founded themselves on the best English colonial models — those of India as portrayed by Kipling.

"They have three or four servants in Manila; back home they would probably have had one, if any. In Manila, they cultivated strutting till it has arrived at the dignity of a fine art. In the little village back home in the States, the little home of yesteryear would have allowed them no room for struts, and their coming and going would have attracted no attention.

"In Manila, with great ostentation, they carry the White Man's Burden. Back home they would have nobody's burdens to carry but their own; and incidentally, nobody in the old town would care very much what they said or what they did. So their strutting and their depictions of white man's supremacy have graduated them into a ridiculous American aristocracy impossible to produce or to perpetuate in the air of the United States."

The words above are not written by a Filipino columnist, but by Sen. Harry B. Hawes, one of the authors of the Hare-Hawes-Cutting Bill that presaged political independence for the Philippines, in his book "The Philippine Uncertainty."

Gov. Gen. Francis B. Harrison who served the Philippines well, in his book, "The Cornerstone of Philippine Independence," also dealt with the evils of this anti-Filipino cabal:

"An active lobby was maintained in the Manila Hotel which seized on each traveler upon his arrival and filled him full of race prejudice and gloom . . .

"On Christmas Eve, a gathering of several dozen ignorant men without arms, mostly of the cook and coachman

44

class . . . were arrested by the city police. This disturbance was heralded in the United States press as an insurrection . . .

"Around the American supper table, the matter went much farther: Every possible story, real or fabricated, which stirred up hatred of or heaped ridicule upon the Filipino people was told there with gusto, and all were probably carried forth and repeated by the patient-looking and apparently uncomprehending Filipino muchachos who waited upon the table . . .

"The prestige of the white man must be maintained at any and all hazards. The Asiatic must not be recognized socially; he must be humble in address and cringe before his master; in fine, he must be kept in his place. Thus were some of the most ancient civilizations of the world held up to hatred, contempt, and ridicule. We cannot wonder that resentment has burnt into the soul of the Asiatic . . ."

And Gov. Gen. William Howard Taft who later became the president of the United States had this to say:

"There are many Americans in these islands, possibly a majority who are strongly opposed to the doctrine of the Philippines for the Filipinos . . . who have the bitterest feeling toward the Filipino and entertain the view that legislation for the benefit of the Filipinos . . . is evidence of a lack of loyalty to the Americans . . . Accordingly, they write the most scurrilous articles impeaching the honesty of Filipino officials . . .

"They resent everything in the government that is not American. They insist that there is a necessity for a firm government here rather than a popular one and that the welfare of Americans and American trade should be regarded as paramount."

Sen. Harry Hawes recounted an incident in the Army and Navy Club wherein some Filipinos "either were thrust upon or deliberately trespassed upon the club. Native waiters were sent to drive them off . . . There were no

45

fights, no arrests, no disorder . . . The story was cabled to America that there had been a riot and American men and women had been stoned. This naturally prompted headlines."

Senator Hawes quoted a newspaper report in the United States describing the incident as the "greatest political demonstration in the history of the Philippine Islands . . . This occurred on the premises of the Army and Navy Club where a mob of 200 swarmed over the lawns and invaded the porches. The demonstrators grew ugly when ordered off by private police and invaded an outdoor swimming pool, stoning army officers, their wives, and children."

Anybody who has ever moved around the "cosmopolitan" cocktail circles or read anti-Filipino news reports from the United States, may find that all these have quite a familiar ring.

———0———

JIM INGERSOLL, ALL-AMERICAN

"Hello, Lord Jim . . . I am Gunga Din" — these words, a hearty handshake and two good laughs opened a new era for Philippine-American economic relations in March of last year.

On the other end of the handshake was James H. Ingersoll, with a rank of minister in the US foreign service, the director of the Agency for International Aid (USAID) operations mission in the Philippines, a duck out of water if there ever was one. For he is neither a career diplomat or a government bureaucrat; he is a businessman on his first government assignment, pressed into service by President John F. Kennedy himself.

On my end of the handshake was also a duck out of water. For I, too, am a businessman on my first government job — then newly appointed to the cabinet as the chairman of the National Economic Council, in charge of economic policy, reparations schedules, tariff rates, and all sources of external funds including UN and US foreign aid and loans.

Even with all the laughs, Jim and I started uncomfortably in our joint administration of American aid and Philippine counterpart funds. For Jim and I were essentially of the "private executive" type, with strong opinions, strong wills of our own, and an even stronger dislike for normal diplomatic niceties. Jim can, with impatience walk out on an important official; and I am a nationalist who would on occasion sarcastically refer to myself as "Gunga Din" to shame the colonials.

Yet, happily enough, as President Macapagal himself noted, never has so much been accomplished in so short a time, in so businesslike a manner and in the spirit of maximum cooperation in the whole field of foreign-aid operations, as in time of Jim's administration of aid funds this year.

In less than a year — during a time of foreign exchange shortage, almost ₱100 million worth of dollars were made available to the government for essential imports without the use of our international reserves; and during a time of tight credit some ₱65 million of peso funds were channeled to developmental purposes through credit agreements and the relaxation of restrictions on industrial loan funds. Even more significant was the use of funds and technical aid in the more meaningful areas of economic planning and development.

Not all Americans are what Filipinos demonstrate or declare a strike against. Some Americans are allright, and certainly Jim Ingersoll is the type of American Filipino nationalists are proud to call a friend. It was because of him and his understanding of the historic forces shaping our nation, that the US aid program has achieved unparalleled success during the last year, and has in a way redeemed the American image from being irretrievably tarnished in the Philippines.

Much of the reason for this lies in the character of Jim Ingersoll. He is an American "internationalist" who is the kindred spirit of the Filipino nationalist, since both stand for the compassion of the strong for the dignity of **the weak nations.** He is an industrialist from **Chicago, a** twin soul of the Filipino industrialist who seeks to deliver his country from feudal stagnation. He is a liberal-educated humanist from the Middle-West who despises the McCarthyist and Klu Klux Klan variety of beachcombers.

He is a businessman with a sure instinct for cutting down bureaucratic red-tape; for seeking out meaningful projects that yield maximum result for the least effort and expenditure; for identifying areas where private business initiative can be exercised most effectively for national economic development. He is every bit what I hope I am on my own side of the fence.

When we first faced each other across the negotiating table, I challenged: "Watch out, Jim, I have been negotiating with American businessmen most of my life. You know as well as I do that negotiation is not an act of love as most Fil-American bureaucrats think it is. Negotiation is a *test of strength* as we businessmen know it is."

And Jim accepted: "I am here to promote American policy. You are here to promote the interest of your own country. Where these two coincide, let's cooperate. Where they conflict, let's fight like hell. Whatever is the outcome, let's bear it with humor and dignity. All right?"

And so over the field of battle that was the negotiating table, Jim and I bargained, blustered, bluffed, shouted, flabbergasted, dared and threatened each other — in an effort to wangle the most concessions from each other.

The bureaucrats and defenders of Bataan could never understand this. Some Americans accused me of bullying tactics and anti-Americanism. Some Filipinos including a cabinet member, accused Jim of being discourteous and anti-Filipino. Jim and I know better.

If the Philippines is now richer by the establishment of a private Economic Development Foundation to help set up new industries and rehabilitate old ones — by the refinancing of capital dry industries through the Industrial Guarantee Loan fund — by the financing of new enterprises by the Private Development Corporation —

If the Philippines is now profiting by the rationalization of the power development program by the same survey team that planned the power grid of Marshall Plan Europe — by the peso financing of a massive electrification program designed to bring light and power to every municipality — by the financing of the completion of 50 large irrigation projects, that have been started, 90 per cent completed and so far abandoned to the elements —

If the Philippines is now benefiting by the many more self-help, community development, and agro-industrial projects through use of agricultural surplus and peso loan funds — by a needed land survey through photogrammetry and fund allocation for agricultural credit in Land Reform Districts — by the text-book program for public schools and in-service teacher training — by loans to such educational institutions as the University of the Philippines — by the veritable flood of surplus vehicles and equipment made available to government bureaus and local governments —

And if the United States has anything at all to be proud of in the Philippines during the last troubled year of reexamination and adjustment in the relations between the two countries —

Then most of the credit belongs to Minister James H. Ingersoll, All-American patriot, who knows as most of other Americans do not, that the interest of the United States is best served by a Philippines which is not a friend in chronic need but a friend indeed — one who, *being independent, can be depended upon.*

Jim Ingersoll leaves his government's service this week to resume his post in his family corporation, the mammoth Borg-Warner industrial complex, one of the largest in the United States.

Goodbye, Lord Jim. No despedida parties to spoil your tummy and waste your time — only this, Jim, to warm your heart and to pass on as a legacy unto your issue:

THANK YOU — from a friend, from President Macapagal, and a grateful nation.

FAREWELL TO ESTERLINE

I am a Filipino nationalist — and I like John H. Esterline, the USIS Director at the American Embassy.

So many unkind things have been written and said of John Esterline. He was accused of having tried to maneuver the Philippine-American Cultural Foundation (Philippine contribution: tax-exemption privileges, ₱10 million worth of government land and a projected ₱4 million in private donations. American contribution: $1 million only) into being an outright American propaganda agency.

He was pilloried as the man who allegedly perpetrated the "bomb-hoax" that pictured Filipinos as would-be-child-killers — an incident that triggered an international press war and a series of demonstrations against the U.S. embassy. Worst of all, he was depicted as a CIA agent spying on and subverting a friendly people.

It was understandable that in this era of resurgent nationalism, John would be fair game for Filipino newsmen. But it was incomprehensible that he would also be an object of derision among a few of his own countrymen in the cocktail circuit.

Who is Dr. John H. Esterline?

I know him well, and I will say this much: He is a better man and a far greater American than any of the detractors among his own countrymen.

John is an American, first and foremost, and he is highly respected as such, even by nationalists. In speaking engagements or cocktail debates, he has been an unabashed and forthright defender of American interests and policies — whether these be completely acceptable to Filipinos or not. And he has the courage to take his lickings for being so, instead of taking refuge under the hypocrisy of being the "blue-eyed redeemer of the unworthy brown race."

He is a rare "Speak-for-yourself John" who never resorted to hiring Filipino spokesmen, or concocting anonymous stories for Washington datelining. Nor does he pull strings and bully his way around; always he personally visits any Filipino, big-shot or small fry, to make his own representations. He never resorted to "Okay, boys, let's contact Secretary x x x and get him to put the heat on Commissioner x x x."

For Dr. John Esterline is a former college professor, a liberal-minded intellectual who is engaged in the great battlefield of ideas — where every idea must meet the challenge of other ideas in open, free and unlimited debate. It is this passion for personal involvement that has made him the most controversial and fascinating American in the Philippines today.

He has organized a series of successful seminars, expanded and improved the facilities of the USIS libraries, and is more to be found in the company of Filipino students, intellectuals, newsmen and nationalists than in the inbred circle of foreign cocktail cowboys.

John and his wife, May, may always be seen with their Filipino friends in movies, plays, musical programs, classical readings, fiestas, and other cultural occasions.

John is a unique American. He is always involved somehow with Pinoys at all levels. At a traffic stop, he would strike up a conversation with the driver of the car next to his and in a matter of minutes make a friend for life. He would accompany newsmen on the President's state visit to the United States, manipulate events so as to effect an unforgettable unscheduled meeting between the two Presidents in San Francisco on a Sunday afternoon — and wax poetic over President Johnson's buss on the cheek of the First Lady.

In the book "Ugly American", whose author Lederer is his friend, John was depicted as one of the good Americans who used a Rolleiflex camera to befriend an intransigent Asian editor — based on actual events that happened between John and Tarzie Vittachi, Ceylon editor, who is a frequent visitor to our shores.

A really rare type of overseas American, John Esterline is humble in speech and manners, loquacious without being pushy, appreciative but not acquisitive or greedy, proud but never arrogant nor condescending — and above all, faithful to one wife all his life.

We Filipino nationalists have a special place in our hearts for guys like John Esterline, unabashed All-American and a liberal democratic intellectual. We met him three years ago, shortly after he took up his local post and long before I joined the President's cabinet. And we — a couple of newsmen, a senator, and I — lost no time initiating him into the fold.

There is an elaborate initiation rite (hazing) we reserve for the very few Americans we fondly welcome to the company of educated Filipinos.

First test: Make him angry.

Question: Oh Esterline, what are you really here for?

Answer: To promote ever closer relations between Mother America and her son the Philippines.

Question: Heavens, wouldn't that be incestuous?

At this point, nine out of ten Americans would yell bloody murder, call in the CIA to apply the water cure on the blasted communists. But not Esterline. He let out a belly laugh that shook the rafters and successfully passed the first test.

Second test: Make him sick.

Question: Hey, Esterline, know what is the greatest riddle of all time? It is this: "Which came first, the chicken or the egg?" Well now, you see before you the answer to that riddle: a *balut*. My friend, you eat a balut and you acquire the wisdom of all the ages, for a balut is *both* the chicken and the egg. Care to try?

This is the acid test only one out of a thousand Americans would even try; and 99 out of a hundred who try, would get laid up for a week pale-green sick with nausea.

But our friend Esterline nonchalantly ate five baluts — soup, chicken, yolk, hard white core and all — smacked his lips and asked for more! In shocked desperation, we handed him a pack of cheap, smelly, black, bitter-sweet Pagkakaisa cigarillos — he didn't smoke them, he ate them too!

A week later, Esterline turned the table on us. He picked out a U.S. marine, trained him, entered him in a balut-eating contest at the Pateros Fiesta — and watched with a toothy grin, as the marine won the contest hands down, swallowing 18 baluts in 5 minutes, face smeared, mouth drooling, nose dripping with what-not — while we Filipinos in the audience turned pale-green and hectic blue, absolutely sick with nausea.

Dr. John H. Esterline is leaving this week for a new assignment in Washington, as Chief, Far East Division for Educational and Cultural Affairs in the State Department.

So long, John, we will miss you. You are a far better American than some of us Filipinos are Filipinos. But you made us act more like Filipinos because by your presence here, you have stimulated thought and galvanized action — which is the function of a truly involved intellectual.

For that, Dr. John H. Esterline — we Filipinos salute you, and fare thee well!

WHY I AM A GIRL SCOUT

No, I am not a girl scout.

But many years ago, I coached a little girl named Heidi Peralta in an oratorical contest in which she won the gold medal (naturally). Her piece which I helped write, is reproduced below as a tribute to my favorite girl scouts — Mrs. Milagros Villasor and the mothers, officials of Girl Scouts of Negros Occidental and the Philippines.

* * * * *

Like every other girl, I struggled a span of years between the ages of 11 to 14 known as the Awkward Age.

It was a time of physical growth — when I could eat all the food I wanted with a reasonable assurance that I would grow upwards and not front-and-sideways.

It was a time of change — when glandular changes transformed me from a tree-climbing skinful of noise into a chair-warming tower of silence, shy, reticent and extremely unsure of myself. I was prone to anxiety, fear, frequent changes of mood and extreme sensitivity to criticism. I was neither woman nor child, and by the way I felt, neither animal, vegetable nor mineral.

It was the time of loneliness — a sort of emotional loneliness that prevailed even in a crowd — a loneliness that exploded into fantastic day-dreams about knights-in-armor and love unrequited — a loneliness that provoked silent tears on my pillow, and an ache in the bosom halfway between agony and ecstancy.

Monsignor Fulton Sheen once said that a teenager is a chick breaking the shell in which she is confined — the shell of the family — and beginning to find herself in a great wide world. Her personality begins to say, "I am me! I am myself! I am not just one of the family, I'm different."

Thus I was when I was 11 years old. I was myself, and I craved recognition.

And so I wrote my name thousands of times on reams of blank paper, practicing the scrawl which was to be my mark upon the world.

And so I insisted that my family call me by my real name and not just "Hoy, Nene!"

And so, when my parents would say, "Let's all go and visit Tia Maria," I would refuse and put up an argument, partly to attract attention, partly to assert my free will and individuality above that collective anonymous group known as "we, the family."

Then I joined the Girl Scouts of the Philippines. I felt a sense of discovery akin to that of stout Cortes as he stood on a peak at Darien. I felt, a new world spreading out before me. As Monsignor Sheen expressed it, I was breaking out of the shell of the family into the great wide world.

That "great wide world" was of course my girl scout troop. This group of 24 girls was indeed my world and universe, the focal point of my existence, in other words, my gang.

We developed a sense of group loyalty that was directed into teamwork, discipline, cooperation, sportsmanship, and above all, a deep sense of responsibility.

The restless and tremendous physical energy, born out of the biological impulses stirring within us, was channeled into such useful activities as sewing and cooking.

But most important of all, I learned from the Girl Scouts that for my ego to assert itself, to be able to say, "I am myself and not somebody else," I must create, not imitate.

Too many teenagers derive release from anonymity through imitation — imitation by hero-worship of a movie star, be she saint or siren; imitation by mimicry of one's companions without being committed to a sense of values or self-restraint; imitation that manifests itself in lipstick, high heels, cigarettes, cha-cha, and fan clubs for no other reason than that "Everybody does it."

A girl scout has to say "No" to certain things. She never fully submits to the mob, because the mob is often wrong. She participates, never imitates. She is no atom of water in a shiftless ocean, she is an important cog in a purposeful machine. She accepts responsibility, no matter how burdensome. She creates, she is creative, and she asserts her individuality before God and man.

These are the reasons why I am a girl scout.

But there are other reasons that extend far beyond my person and my age, and embrace the whole nation and future generations.

Today, in the midst of a world torn asunder by conflicting ideologies, under a constant cloud of atomic war that threatens to obliterate mankind, our own country, the Philippines, is trying to assert itself as a nation — even as I tried to assert myself as an individual in the late stages of my childhood.

Like me, the Philippines is undergoing the span of years known as the Awkward Age, trying to be politically independent while economically insecure; tending toward imitation of Mother America for the sake of imitation, yet trying to assert its own uniqueness and individuality as a nation, beset on one hand by reactionaries and carpet-baggers who would turn the clock back to feudalism and economic stagnation, and on the other, by radicals who would advocate political upheaval by violence and bloodshed. Like me, the Philippines is every bit as prone to anxiety, fear, frequent changes of mood and sensitivity to criticism as I ever was in my Awkward Age.

Our instability as a nation is engendered by the wide chasm that separates men of extreme wealth and men of extreme poverty. We need a middle class — a new generation of financially and intellectually independent men

57

imbued with the qualities of industry, thrift, honesty, self-restraint, self-reliance, discipline, initiative, imagination and talent for organization — qualities ingrained in every true Girl Scout.

God grant that we, Girl Scouts of the Philippines, as the future mothers of our country, out of our wombs and by the power of our example, bring forth this new generation — a generation that may yet make the Philippines prosperous and great, respected among nations and a power for the greater good of all mankind.

PRODUCTIVITY IN FREEDOM*

In a dark time of England's history, Winston Churchill said:

"Come then — let us to the task, to the battle and the toil — each to our part, each to our stations . .... Let us go forward together in all parts of the land. There is not a week, nor a day, nor an hour to be lost."

We in Asia live in a different time of perilous challenge. But these words are no less meant for us who are now engaged in a pressing war against poverty.

Our problem is not only that we have so little; our problem is that we have yet to do so much. We want much, we need much for Asia's millions, and while we can count on some assistance from those who have conquered want, we must yet rely on ourselves, on our efforts, on the fruits of our own strenuous labors.

Any decisive advance in Asia must come from Asians. There is no other way. That is our destiny as free men — if we desire to remain free.

Hence, the special urgency of the symposium that we have just closed. It has presented the Asian problem in the only realistic way: in human terms. In the past few days, we have emphasized *human resources* as Asia's most important, most decisive resource in meeting the challenge of modern development.

Indeed, this is the truth in Asia, that human labor is the creator of wealth. This is, however, but the passing truth in industrialized societies.

---

* Speech of Chairman Hilarion M. Henares, Jr. prepared for the closing ceremonies of the Asian Productivity Organization Symposium on August 24, 1965.

Age of Machines

The industrialized societies of the world are on the threshold of a machine economy, while we have yet to make our human economies function as they should. In the United States, for example, automation is displacing human labor. With cybernation, man may yet be totally submerged by thinking machines in the production of his needs.

These scientific developments pose strange and complicated challenges to man. They are bound to require their own economic theories, their own social orders, and who knows, their particular politics.

The possibilities are exciting, perilous, and breathless. What will humanity be like in an automated, cybernated economy? Will men be some kind of neo-Periclean Greeks who philosophize under the elms while machine slaves do the work of society for them?

But exciting, perilous, and breathless as the possibilities may be, we in Asia must, in the long interval, consider the all-too-human dimensions.

We must yet rely on our sinews, on the agility of our brains and the tolerance of our bodies. In trying to produce more, we must see to it that more and more of us must produce.

That is the crucial question.

Aftermath of Revolution

We are experiencing the classic aftermath of revolution. We have achieved our political freedom, but we had to pay a high price for it. The price was neglect of the non-political aspects of nationhood. For centuries, our collective obsession was to spawn agitators, revolutionaries, and charismatic leaders. These were men of words and men of political action.

We did not have enough, if at all, of administrators, skilled workers, and even independent entrepreneurs who must take over the machinery of government and the economy.

The task was to produce heroes and revolutionaries; but the time has come for those who must do the chores of national life.

Our situation, unfortunately, has no Western parallels. America became independent at a time when she had enough men of wisdom and skill to manage their affairs. As a matter of fact, they defended their control of their national affairs against the political and economic impositions of their mother country, England. The American Revolution was, in a sense, a coup.

As for the French Revolution, it was the revolution of a vital, actually controlling class against royalty.

Only in the terrifying examples of the Russian and Chinese revolutions do we see the parallel of a so-called liberated people wresting in their hands the control and direction of national life. In their consolidation of their proletarian revolutions, the Soviet and Chinese leaders have to whip their people into moving forward. Traditional freedoms were sacrificed for the glory of a ruthless and regimented economy.

The revolutionary state demanded all, and all were conscripted to its service.

Do these communist examples, then, have some lessons for us?

Let us approach this question with fear and trembling.

The Problem of Work

The problem, it is said, is not only how to provide work, but also, and more important, how to make people work as a matter of course. In effect, the question is how to foster an ethic of effort, a morality of work.

There are probably naturally indolent peoples, as colonizers of old days used to point out, but I personally doubt it. Indolence is the quality of those who see no pur-

61

pose, no meaning, in their labor. Let us grant that in the West, work has the status of a personal code of honor, the strong influence of a mystique.

I must grant that we have not had this in Asia, with the possible exception of Japan. We have not had it because somehow in colonial times, it was a mark of our identity and protest not to exert too much, for the surplus of our efforts would redound not to us but to the colonial master.

This explains the seeming lack of dedication, the indifference towards that extra push, the tendency to pause among our peoples. There are exceptions, to be sure, mostly in industry, but there are areas outside of the vital center in which the slow pace of centuries has been encrusted in the popular mind.

It is not enough to deplore this. The essential thing is to understand it.

Soviet Russia and China understood it in a totally different way. These communist states made production a national morality, and the unproductive was regarded as something of a criminal. The definite solution was forced labor.

But since we abhor this method, being free men, we need an alternative. It may be — this is just a guess — the moral equivalent of the Great Wall of China, to the building of which millions of lives have been offered by ruthless authority. What, then, must we build in order to harness the vast reservoir of energy that is within the nerves and sinews of Asian masses? There cannot be many Aswan dams, however. Much of the work that must be accomplished are not giant highways but thousands of comparatively tiny feeder roads. How does one summon enthusiasm in the performance of everyday tasks?

The Sense of Freedom

We can say, higher wages, less working hours, and more leisure. But we shall be lying, and we cannot be credible. For we know that these boons are somewhat at the end of the road of strenuous labor. In Asia, we shall labor much before these can be achieved in significant measure. We know that there will be times when the road seems to lengthen, when we seem to be deceived by our vision.

The fruits of productivity come, perhaps, in a decade — at the most, half a decade. Meanwhile, we feel like Sisyphus, endlessly and meaninglessly laboring to take the giant boulder at the top of the mountain, after which it will slide down again, and we must push it up once more, again and again.

The ends of a free society are different from a totalitarian one. Where the latter can harness everybody to task by stipulating that so much blood, sweat and tears will mean an atom bomb after ten years, or so many missile silos, the former must frame its appeal less belligerently. Besides, only harnessed peoples will work for an atom bomb. Free spirits have a different scale of values.

I said "free spirits," and in that may lie our appeal. The crucial problem is how to develop the ethic of effort, the morality of work, as an indispensable price of freedom.

At this outset, the appeal sounds very abstract, too obtuse, for the man who is too worried about his stomach to worry about freedom. But that observation merely means that the task of orientation is difficult. It is not impossible.

I believe that we in the APO are beginning something of that appeal. Much of our discussions are technical to be sure, but a great deal can also be channeled along ideological lines.

I do not mean that productivity must have the messianic aura of an anti-communist crusade. I simply mean that free men must realize in our time and place that they are fated to work, to exert, to aspire, to achieve, for the very simple reason that they are free.

To be free is to be responsible for one's self.

A Beginning

At least, more and more Asians are beginning to realize this. Fascinated by the Chinese experiment, they ask themselves whether the same results can be achieved in free societies. My answer is "yes." It only remains for us to do what as a matter of course 600 million Chinese do under compulsion.

It remains for us to discipline ourselves. Against the collective discipline of the blue ants, we can put up the voluntary self-discipline of free men.

I believe we are making an important beginning. Let us not falter.

Let us to the task, to the battle and to the toil. There is not a moment to lose.

Did not Nehru say that in Asia, you have to run just to stand still? But if we run long enough, we shall move.

PART II

ON ECONOMICS

I read practically all the leading articles on economic studies and I recall distinctly that among the articles that I read there stood out as exemplary in their sense, in their learning, and in their intelligence the articles of one who is truly one of the authorities in economics in our country — Hilarion M. Henares, Jr.

PRESIDENT OF THE PHILIPPINES

INDUSTRIALIZATION AND NATIONALISM*

I am deeply privileged by this occasion to speak on two subjects which have not only been of long, personal obsession, but which today constitute the two driving passions of this nation.

Contemporary developments attest only too clearly to the ascendancy which both the *industrial* and the *nationalistic* movements in this country have finally achieved in the national consciousness, making of them the pervasive influence that they have become in the councils of public policy.

What we are in fact witnessing today is the growing rapport and interdependence between the forces of the industrial movement, on the one hand, and the forces of the nationalist crusade, on the other hand, a rapport and interdependence made inevitable by the logic of necessity, and confrontation with the common enemy.

For both these movements had been from their infancy the target of colonial suppression.

From the day that the United States Congress enacted the Philippine Tariff Law and the Payne-Aldrich Act in 1909, *imposing* upon the Philippines a relationship of *free trade* with the United States, the industrial movement in this country was condemned to failure.

As former Central Bank Governor Miguel Cuaderno said, in his famous brief arguing for the revision of the Bell Trade Act, the Philippine Tariff Act of 1909 and the Payne-Aldrich Act "resulted in the Philippines becoming dependent upon the United States", for these Acts, as Governor Cuaderno succinctly explained, simply meant that

---

*Speech delivered by Hilarion M. Henares, Jr., Chairman of the National Economic Council, at a University Convocation sponsored by the U. P. College of Business Administration & School of Economics, Abelardo Hall, U. P., Diliman. March 10, 1965.

"American goods were to enter the Philippines duty-free and without quantitative limitations."

These Acts of colonial imposition were vigorously protested in the United States Congress by the then Filipino Resident Commissioner, Benito Legarda. As Governor Cuaderno narrated, the Resident Commissioner argued, with almost prophetic insight, that the provisions of the Payne-Aldrich and Philippine Tariff Acts "would distort the economic development of the Philippines and imperil the Filipinos' desire for independent existence, and that it would cause balance-of-payments difficulties." That was in 1909, fifty-six years ago.

Unlimited entry of American industrial products free of tariff made impossible even the rudimentary beginnings of industrialization in this country.

While the Philippine government was subsequently given power in 1916 thru the Jones Act to enact its own tariff law, that same law decreed that the trade relations between the Philippines and the United States shall continue to be governed exclusively by the Congress of the United States which meant the right of American business interests to export to the Philippines, without limitation as to quantity, industrial products free of duty.

Again, as Governor Cuaderno pointed out in his admirable brief, "since all United States articles were admitted free of duty into the Philippines, the imposition of customs duty on foreign goods resulted in a preferential trade advantage for such United States articles as were imported into the Philippines."

American colonial policy, in other words not only suppressed Filipino industrialization, but *definitely oriented Philippine trade to American goods, diverting us away from the potentialities of other markets.*

The free trade arrangement between the Philippines and the United States, as you know, subsisted until the outbreak of the Second World War. After that war, free trade was resumed for another period of 8 years, from 1946 to 1954. Resumption of this iniquitous relationship was made under the strength of the Bell Trade Act of 1946 which the United States Congress enacted a few months just before Philippine independence. Parenthetically, that act not only reimposed free trade upon the Philippines for another 8 years, but likewise contained the infamous Parity Provision, acceptance of which was made the condition precedent to the grant of war damage compensation.

One sees, therefore, that it was not until *1954* that the Philippine economy was relieved of a "special relationship" designed to suppress, as it was able to suppress, the industrial movement in this country.

As Dr. Salvador Araneta, in whose spirit and achievements are embodied the aspiration of the economic nationalists of today, said on one occasion of his debates with the late President Roxas on the issue of the Bell Trade Act:

> "Free trade means no industrialization for the Philippines. It means a backward Philippines that will be little more than an economic dependency of the United States — serving in that regard the function of a vegetable garden to an industrial state, such as the Nazis had planned to make of France with respect to Germany." (Economic Reexamination of the Philippines, p. 100).

The American assault against the industrial movement in the Philippines, however, did not end with the termination of free trade in 1954.

We are indebted to the late Senator Claro M. Recto for a masterful analysis and exposure of post-war American economic policy in the Philippines.

In a documented analysis of America's post-war colonial policy, the late Senator Recto, in a speech before the Philippine Columbian Association on September 26, 1956, exposed what he termed "the powerful economic reasons behind American actuations" in this country, which were, to secure the Philippines as a perpetual source of America's raw material requirements, and to prevent underdeveloped economies from competing with American manufacturers.

The late Senator disclosed that during the *1955* session of Congress, the Philippine Congress, if you will, an alien inspired legislation was introduced which would have committed the Philippines to a national policy that would maintain for the Filipinos an agricultural economy for all times. This, on the face of a policy declaration by the National Economic Council at that time decreeing industrialization as the basic economic policy for the Philippines.

Congress, alerted opportunely, frustrated the measure.

I have taken your time briefly reviewing the background against which the Philippine industrial movement has developed in order to place in full perspective the challenges which this movement faces at present, and to enable us to appreciate the reasons behind the increased rapport between the Filipino industrialists, on the one hand, and the nationalist theoreticians, on the other hand.

For the industrial movement today continues under the assault of the very colonial forces which, for the last fifty years, have tried to suppress it. Only this time, the assault has taken a substantially different form, and is prompted by a substantially different objective.

That assault consists in riding on the industrial movement, with the ostensible objective of dominating it. Having failed to repress it, they now seek to conquer it.

I conjure no imagined or fancied threat. No less than the three ranking Filipino trade and industry organization, namely, the Philippine Chamber of Industries, the Chamber of Commerce of the Philippines, and the National Economic Protectionism Association, have been stirred by this sense of common peril, prompting them recently to file a joint petition with my office urging the United States government to relinquish the parity rights of its citizens in the Philippines even before the scheduled expiry of the Laurel-Langley Agreement in 1974

In the thinking of the Philippine Chamber of Industries, parity must be repealed immediately because ten more years of it could place vital sectors of the national economy in the hands of non-Filipinos.

This is an organization composed of at least 500 industrial Filipino firms. The apprehension which they collectively voiced is not something we can lightly dismiss.

This, of course, merely echoes the long, bitter but isolated protest of the nationalists when they fought their losing but valiant battle against the post-war colonialism in early 1946.

But today, an emergent entrepreneurial class, spawned by the era of controls, has given Nationalism in this country a depth of support which was not there before, has given it a militant soldiery, so to speak, thus giving the nationalist cause a base far broader in scope than the sheer intellectualism and professionalism, and I use professionalism in a complementary sense, that so far have characterized it.

This is what industrialization has done for nationalism.

But the war has just begun. In the years ahead, we shall see this war intensified, and this will be fought in corporate suits, in the battlefield of the securities market, in the entire gamut of the competitive arena.

Already, the first Filipino-controlled petroleum refinery has yielded to the colonial assault. And there have been many more such corporate surrenders in the brief period since the protective mantles of control were removed in 1962, largely because of Congressional failure to enact substitutive protective measures and the failure of the Central Bank credit policy to respond to the new requirements of Filipino industries under the era of decontrol and the imperatives of growth and competition for the domestic market against established foreign companies.

The trend and logic are clear. The colonial policy from 1909 to 1954 was to make of the Philippines an extension of a foreign economy, with this sovereign republic to serve

71

as a source of raw material and a market for industrial products.

Now that industrialization has become inevitable, the colonial strategy is obviously to assume control and direction of the industrial movement thru the direct investment process which Senator Recto had consistently warned the country against during his lifetime.

The socio-economic program of the Administration anticipated such a move and that is why the program made amply clear from the start that it is committed to the objective that Filipinos are to be the chief determinants and principal beneficiaries of their country's progress.

This statement of objective, however, is in urgent need of administrative and legislative implementation, particularly in the face of the massive assault by the colonial forces upon the delicate fabric of our young industrial structure.

What is needed are implementing policies that would keep the new colonialism at bay, confine it to such pioneer areas of economic activity where it is needed, under conditions of partnership with Filipinos, and prevent it from intruding into those areas where the Filipino entrepreneur has already established himself.

It is in the light of these exigencies that the National Economic Council last year passed a resolution declaring wholly-owned foreign subsidiaries to be inimical to the national interest, and urging Congress to withhold from this particular form of corporate enterprise any incentive or statutory guarantees to investment.

For, in my view, wholly-owned or foreign controlled subsidiaries constitute a corporate colonialism that is an affront to the sensibilities and aspirations of a sovereign republic. In the words of President Macapagal, delivered before the American Chamber of Commerce of the Philippines, these subsidiaries "reflect a policy of exclusion in reverse, directed by the guest against the very nationals of the host country".

72

By the same token, and upon vigorous protest by Filipino businessmen against the entry of two American corporate giants into the cement industry, the National Economic Council passed public condemnation upon the practice of foreign investors in muzzling into industries pioneered in and established by Filipinos.

The NEC resolutions, however, have at most a suasive effect upon the actuations of the new colonialism. There are no legal sanctions which would render these resolutions legally effective.

What is needed is legislation that would establish the ground rules, for without these we have a frontier that is open to the same colonizing spirit and drive that wrested the Americas from the Indians.

But even more paramount than legislation, since legislation cannot fully achieve the purposes of protectionism as long as parity exists, is the need to consolidate the rapport between the nationalist forces and the entrepreneurial class into an enduring alliance.

For the nationalists, whether student, professional, laborer and academician — and the recent public demonstrations against parity and the base killings have demonstrated that their number is legion — this means vigilantly fighting the cause of the Filipino entrepreneur for economic hegemony, and openly supporting the entrepreneurial class on the many issues bearing on this objective.

For the Filipino entrepreneur, this means lending the full weight of his support to the nationalist movement, even in those aspects of it which are only remotely connected with the Filipino's fight for economic preeminence in his own country.

Let the new entrepreneur and the old nationalist find, not only solace in each other's cause, but also strength.

In this, the great battle of our times, no Filipino can afford to assume a posture of non-involvement without appearing incongruous.

We are engaged in nothing less than the fight for the economic independence of our people in their own land, and if this fight has not assumed the same dramatic coloring as that which attended the debates on the Hare-Hawes-Cutting Law and the Tydings Act, it is because the fight for economic hegemony is normally a less colorful one than the fight for political freedom. But that does not detract from the supreme significance of its outcome upon the integrity and sovereignty of a country that pretends to be free.

It is for this reason that I take strong exception to the published views of an eminent citizen and former Cabinet member in a previous Liberal Administration* when he charged that all this agitation for the early repeal of parity is nothing more but the empty posturing of professional patriots.

I believe that such statement reflects a mind that has become insulated from the times, insensitive to the urgencies which face the Filipinos today, and unmindful of the supreme indignity to the national pride which parity continuingly represents.

As a proud citizen of this sovereign Republic, concerned by the threats of economic colonialism, I urge the early repeal of parity through bilateral consent, even if this means renegotiating the Laurel-Langley Agreement for the purpose.

For parity is the *wedge* with which the colonial forces seek to perpetuate their policies and objectives in this country, dividing our people, and rendering it impossible for our own government to delineate strategic areas of economic activity exclusive for its own citizens.

Let the controversy on the Retail Trade Nationalization Act furnish the example.

Parity precisely constituted the colonial string, along with free trade, to America's aid and rehabilitation pro-

---

* Now hired as a member of the Board of Directors of a giant American company.

gram for the Philippines, a condition which, significantly, she did not exact from the numerous other countries who became the beneficiaries of her aid program, and this includes Japan, her former enemy in the Pacific.

And it is parity, subsequently expanded in 1954 to all forms of business activity, which now constitutes the iniquitous armor that insures the new colonialism against such protective measures which our now sovereign government may elect to assert on behalf of the Filipino industrial class.

Knowing the onerous and shameful circumstances under which parity was conceived and imposed, aware of the threat which it poses to the hegemony of our own Filipino industrial class, I feel it the incumbent duty of every Filipino to agitate for its early repeal. By this, I do not refer solely to the parity provision under Article VI of the Laurel-Langley Agreement which a high ranking U.S. official has said that the United States government does not intend to extend beyond 1974. I refer to the parity rights embodied in Article VII of the Laurel-Langley Agreement which confers upon U.S. citizens national treatment in all phases of economic activity in this country with the exception of the exploitation of the natural resources and the operation of public utilities. ·

We are *renegotiating* the Bases Agreement to remove those provisions which infringe upon our sovereignty. There is no reason why the Laurel-Langley Agreement should not be renegotiated for the same purpose.

Industrialization and nationalism — these are the twin passions of our times, for they comprise the two movements which *alone* can catapult our people to economic independence, once the distant dream of our constitutional architects. Separately developed, pursued independently of each other, these two movements will not bring us closer to the national objective, but instead will divide our people, and plunge them to bitter if not enduring differences.

But pursued jointly, one supporting the other, they constitute the kind of amalgam which can produce revolutions — for us, an industrial revolution, by the Filipinos and for the Filipinos. And it is time for such a revolution now. ————o————

WHAT IS THE NORMAL ECONOMY?

When a body is ailing, what is called for is a doctor of medicine.

When the economy is ailing, then what is called for is a doctor of economics, or a plain economist.

Medical doctors may disagree about the cause of the body disease, but there is one thing they absolutely agree on — and that is the normal state to which the human body must be restored.

No medical doctor would reshape the normal human body to accommodate an extra leg for improved locomotion, or a third eye to provide rear-view vision. It just isn't done.

Yet economists would do just that. Economists may disagree as to the cause of the economic malady — but they disagree even more passionately on the final "normal" state to which the economy should be shaped.

What is the "Normal Economy?"

Communism? Socialism? Welfare State? Capitalism? Smithsonian or Keynesian? Planned economy or unfettered free enterprise? Economic protectionism or free trade? Self-sufficiency, interdependence or colonial dependence?

What is considered normal by one economist is often regarded as abhorrently abnormal by another. What one economist looks upon as a paragon of perfection like Marilyn Monroe, another economist may find as revolting as Frankenstein's monster. One Goldwaterite wag once said of Kennedy's New Frontier economics: He cuts off the left ear, then the right ear and grafts on a "new front-ear."

In the Philippines, there is at least some agreement on the kind of economy we do not want. We reject the

76

Marxist Communist concept of a coercive state who owns all means of production, plans everything and orders everyone to conform. Similarly, we reject the Fascistic concept of a corporate state with an all-powerful dictator heading a military-industrial complex.

We pay lip-service to Capitalism with social welfare features, and Free Enterprise within a framework of planned incentives and regulatory restrictions. But these are vague and broad outlines within which there is room for disagreement among our economists and national planners.

Gerald Wilkinson, a British businessman doing business here, recently made a speech saying in effect that we Filipinos should not quarrel with foreigners over how the "economic pie" should be shared. What really matters, he said, is how to make the economic pie big enough for everybody to share. His "advice" is understandable and every Filipino should take it in the spirit in which it is given.

But Wilkinson misses the point. The big quarrel is not so much how to share the pie or how to make it bigger. The big quarrel, to start with, is on what kind of pie to bake — for far too many cooks are spoiling for a mud-pie, a pie-in-the-face farce, or a pie-in-the-sky scheme.

There are at least three major schools of thought on this matter, represented by three powerful economic forces that are now competing in the field of ideas and political power to beat into shape the future of our nation.

These forces are: (1) the Colons (2) the Landed Aristocrats, and (3) the Middle Class. But these labels are misleading.

The Colons are definitely a small but powerful minority. They do not include the majority of foreigners in our midst who sympathize with our national aspirations, who came to help in joint business ventures, in charity foundations and religious institutions, in the Peace Corps or in the USAID and United Nations organizations.

77

The Colons are the few remnants of what Senator Harry Hawes contemptuously wrote about in his book "The Philippine Uncertainty" — who once said "We are here by right of conquest," and who consistently conspired against the grant of our independence — who envision our country as a colonial trading post and an instrument of their Manifest Destiny, and who now use their economic power to preserve their extra-territorial colonial privileges against the higher interest of the great American nation.

The Landed Aristocracy is also a mislabel. For it includes only those whose interests lie in the perpetuation of a feudal type of plantation economy based on privileged raw material exports. It does not include the rice and corn producers, the citrus and coffee growers, and many farmers who cater to domestic consumption.

The Middle Class includes not only factory owners and industrial workers and the people who work in the related fields of distribution, finance, etc., but also professionals (doctors, lawyers, educators and others) of all types, agricultural producers for domestic processing and consumption, and the many foreigners who respect our national aspirations.

Each of these three forces have separate destinies to pursue, although a few persons in each group have the sense of history and the grand design to realize this most crucial fact.

If the Colons had their way, the Philippines of the future will assume the shape of Hawaii, Puerto Rico or Hongkong — a sort of white man's paradise with quaint and happy natives to provide the labor and entertainment.

To achieve this, they want parity rights extended to all foreigners, absolute free trade with industrialized nations and unfettered free enterprise of the type that spawned robber barons, monopolies and great economic depressions.

If the Landed Aristocrats had their way, the Philippines of the future will assume the shape of a Brazil, New

Zealand, or pre-Civil War American South — a nation dominated by feudal overloads with a one-or-two crop economy at the mercy of unpredictable world markets.

To achieve this, they advocate a continuation of a quota-limited export market even at the expense of national sovereignty; privileged exemption from the provisions of the Land Reform Code; exemption from an increased minimum wage, duties and taxes; and straight-jacket laws of every conceivable contrivance based on the proposition that industrialization is a conspiracy against the consumer.

If the Middle Class had its way, the Philippines may in the future be another Japan, United States, or a Prussia among the Germanies.

It advocates nationalism as a copious source of mass enthusiasm for the sacrifices and united action needed to transform a nation and renovate a stagnant society.

It advocates economic protectionism to allow Filipinos the time and patience to develop their industrial skills, mobilize savings and generate capital formation — and bring about an industrial revolution which will in turn bring into the fore a preponderant middle class that will guarantee the stability of our democratic way of life.

It advocates the kind of internationalism and multilateral trade that would make of the Philippines, not a satellite of great powers, but a leader among equals, the dominant partner in Southeast Asian community consisting of Malaysia, Indonesia, Thailand, and others — such dominance to stem not from military might, but from the leadership of the most literate, the most cultured, the most industrialized, the most economically advanced, the most politically mature and the most stable of all nations in this part of the world.

We Filipinos are indeed at the crossroads of our history. We live in a time of change comparable to that of Japan under the reign of Emperor Meiji, of Germany under Bismarck, of America during the Civil War period, of England during the repeal of the Corn Laws.

Our economists and national leaders are beating into shape our future economy — to whatever "normal" shape it must eventually be molded — and with it the ultimate destiny of the Filipino people.

Into the crucible with you all, the Filipino nation is in the making.

THEY WHO NEED, WE WHO WANT

There are many of those who *need* foreign investment, as a woman *needs* a man.

There are few of us who *want* foreign investment, as a man *wants* a woman.

And there is a hell and heaven of a difference between the two. For a woman must dream and wait till the right man comes along; a man ranges far and wide to seek, sample and select. A woman if she is to be honorable, must have a one and only love; a man if he is to be honored, must boast of many loves. A woman serves; a man rules. A woman gives; a man takes. And when the time comes for tearful parting, it is always the woman who is left holding the bag.

How feminine are those who need foreign investment! Like a teen-age girl with a crush, they dream of foreign investment as a knight-in-armor coming to rescue them from economic stagnation. Destined to be dependent and desperately looking for a meal ticket, they look upon foreign capital as the answer to all the country's ills, the patron saint of all economic and social progress — to whom homage requires the unholy sacrifice of the mass of their own domestic capital.

We who want foreign investment are more masculine in our attitude; for being independent, we depend on our own domestic capital for economic development. As the 5-year Socio-Economic Program puts it, "Filipino citizens shall be the chief determinants and the principal beneficiaries of economic progress. We shall welcome all foreign assistance that does not wrest from us our supremacy over our own economic affairs."

We want foreign investment to supplement but not to supplant local capital. We specially want them in areas of endeavor where Filipino capital is neither willing nor able to enter. But we do not want them to establish a monopoly here that might have been subject to anti-trust action in their own country.

We want foreign investment to stimulate and not to overwhelm local enterprises — stimulating them by healthy competition to render better service and produce better goods at cheaper prices.

We want foreign investment as partners but not as masters. We welcome them primarily as loans, and secondarily as joint ventures. For we feel that reputable foreign companies seeking Filipino partners, can do much to induce our citizens to invest idle capital and participate in our country's economic development. We share President Macapagal's misgivings about those who practice "exclusion in reverse against nationals of the host country."

And being manly, we want to seek, sample and select foreign investment from all countries — not only from the United States but also from Japan, Australia, France, Great Britain, Germany and others. Being gentlemen, we would like to treat all with equal respect, and not scandalously favor one over the others.

But those who need foreign investment, like a woman in love, prefer one country and one country alone — giving their all in the name of parity and special relations — and all, because of sentimentally shared memories of war and "liberation." They are resigned to be a ward and an exclusive market — forgetting that the contract expires in 1974 and that the time must come to look for other friends on honorable terms. They refuse to accept the fact that their favorite partner is determined to end the relationship, and has unequivocally and publicly expressed the policy of "multilateral free trade" under the multinational General Agreement on Tariffs and Trade (GATT).

Then like a woman scorned, they unleash a fury such as hell never knew, because they have given too much ($215.7 million in dividends and remittances from 1950 to 1960) and received so little ($19.2 million in investments during the same period). Manly reason, not womanly emotion, might have told them that an investment is a one-shot proposition, while profit outflow is a continuous stream. And oh, such trantrums over the bases question and parity rights — signs of approaching spinsterhood.

We who want foreign investment know from manly experience that the interest of a foreign investor, like a lover's appetite, is whetted by the knowledge of being wanted but not sorely needed. Those who, in desperate need and cloying obeisance, throw themselves at the feet of their foreign lovers, inevitably invite annoyance to the point of frigidity.

Thus parity rights and special relations never enticed the many foreign investors who passionately knock loud and long at the half-closed doors of protectionist Japan and the European Common Market.

We who want foreign investment, want them to serve the cause of Filipino entrepreneurship and advance the course of Philippine industrialization. For it is our dream to see the rise of an indigenous industrial middle class made up of factory owners, workers and professionals — to stride the gap between the idle rich and the jobless poor, to give stability to our democratic way of life, and usher our people from benighted centuries of feudal stagnation into the light of day of modern industrial progress and enlightenment.

We are afraid that those in need may settle too soon for an enclave of prosperous foreigners amidst a sea of economically frustrated Filipinos — a situation that may call for a Fidel Castro, or a Ben Bella. If such an eventuality comes to pass, the foreigners have only their property to lose — but we Filipinos may lose our lives and freedom as well.

Then we all shall have cause to weep. And we shall weep with the anathema of history on our heads, as told in the words of Athrea, mother of weeping Boabdil, exiled king of Granada, when she said:

"Weep like a woman for the loss of the kingdom you did not defend like a man!"

OUR CONDITIONED REFLEX

Now, there's that joke about Mike the Irishman and his wife Maggie.

Mike was an Irishman from the tip of his tongue to the pit of his stomach — which means that he was given to drinking whisky and carousing with the boys every night after dinner. At midnight, he usually staggered home and headed straight for the kitchen sink, when in a fit of drunken nausea, he threw up his evening's meal.

His wife Maggie kept nagging him: "Mike, one of these days, you are going to throw up your guts!" And Mike would answer, "Impossible, impossible."

Well, one night, Maggie was disemboweling a freshly killed chicken, and feeling too tired to clean up, she left the entrails of the chicken in the kitchen sink.

As usual, Mike staggered home at midnight and headed straight for the kitchen sink. Silence. Then a scream, "Maggie!"

Maggie called out, "What happened, Mike?"

Mike answered: "It happened, Maggie, exactly the way you said it would happen! I threw up my guts. *But by the grace of God and with the help of a long spoon, I got 'em all back in!*"

The story reminds me of the joke that is perpetually being played on us by a small group of foreign colons who keep nagging us: "One of these days, if you take away our colonial privileges, you will scare away foreign investment."

We Filipinos are being goaded into a state of mind wherein we can very well, by the grace of God and with the help of a long spoon, swallow hook, line, and sinker the unwholesome and lethal aspects of racial discrimina-

84

tion, monopolistic cartels, parity rights, extra-territorial privileges and the perpetuation of a foreign dominated "colonial trading post" economy that has kept our country in feudal stagnation for the past 400 years.

All these years, we have been systematically subjected to a mass psychological treatment that makes us react like laboratory rats in the manner of Pavlov's conditioned reflex. Whenever some foreigner says, "Hoy, you're scaring away foreign capital!" gongs clang in the cranium, glands secrete their juices, and suddenly, "Oh Judgment, Thou art fled to brutish beasts and men have lost their reason!" . . . and predictably, we are subdued into a mute hypnotic stupor, to endure once more the age-old colonial injustices that need desperately to be corrected if we are to proceed with our nation-building.

Thus we have been led like sacrificial lambs into granting foreigners parity rights which no self-respecting nation has ever done; into extending monopoly rights to foreign cartels that keep life-saving drugs out of the reach of our masses; into suffering the indignities of racial discrimination in pay scales in foreign subsidiaries; into allowing foreign banks an intolerable competitive advantage over our own banks — all because some smart aleck happens to yell "Hoy, you're scaring away foreign capital!" at the right psychological moment.

And all the while, countries like Japan, India, and France, which never yielded to parity rights, foreign monopoly, racial discrimination, or extra-territorial privileges, have been accepting and rejecting a hundred times more foreign capital than the poor Philippines ever hoped to attract.

Sensible and emotionally stable Filipinos will do well to recognize three basic facts of economic life:

First, foreign investors like ordinary people, are a varied lot — ranging from very good to very bad, with varying motivations and predispositions — *and not any one of them is authorized to speak for the others.*

Second, while many countries compete to attract foreign capital, *foreign investors compete even more fiercely with each other to capture the market of any given country.*

Third, *no free and sovereign country ever depended exclusively on foreign investment for its economic development.* No cliche can hide these facts — by the last tax census, of the total net worth of investments in this country, only 2 per cent belong to foreigners, out of which a measly 1.2 per cent belong to American citizens; only 3 per cent of the entire capital requirements of our ambitious 5-year socio-economic program is expected to come from foreign investments.

Somebody from Caltex Philippines, Inc., now being accused of racial discrimination against Filipino executives, was reported to have said that the Tañada bill against discrimination would "scare away foreign investment." He presumes too much on our "conditioned reflex."

Caltex Philippines does not speak for all foreign investors, not any more than Suez Canal Co. in Egypt, United Fruit Co. in Latin America, Union Miniere in Belgian Congo, the Diamond Trust in Africa, or the British East India Company represent the business interests of the industrial nations of the West.

In the Philippines, a majority of foreign investors have set up business in full accordance with the legitimate national aspirations of the Filipino people. They come in joint ventures with Filipino citizens, maintain a maximum of one or two foreign treaty-traders, never treat Filipinos like Negroes, nor intrude upon centers of political influence with offensive familiarity.

They are, among others: Goodrich Rubber, Rohm and Haas, Reynolds Metals, Shell Oil, Sherwin Williams, Sinclair Paints, Eternit Corporation, Union Carbide, Reichhold Chemicals, Wyeth International, Krupp Steel, United Carbon, Westinghouse Electric Corp., General Electric Co., Archer-Midland-Daniels, Rheem, and others — whose combined assets and collective respect for the Filipino far outweigh those of the remaining outposts of corporate colonialism, even with Harry Stonehill thrown in for good measure.

86

EQUAL PAY FOR EQUAL WORK

One of the nightmares that continually haunts Filipinos with any sense of history is that the Philippines may someday be caught in the cross-currents of racial strife. This is specially of serious concern to us when racial prejudice is directed against us by our own guests who are supposed to be our friends.

The lessons of Egypt, Angola, Kenya, Congo and Algeria are too recent to be forgotten. In every case there was a prosperous enclave of foreigners amidst a sea of economic frustration; a rising nationalist movement dammed to the full by stupid attempts to preserve colonial privileges; and then, inevitably, a man of destiny who releases the floodgates of racial resentment on a wave of bloody revolution.

The tragedy is that while the foreigners had only their properties to lose, the poor natives are apt to lose their lives and freedom as well.

Race prejudice dies hard, even in the Philippines. But our fortune lies in the fact that there are always some Filipinos who refuse to be second class citizens in their own country — who denounce, as they did many times in the past, the refusal of foreigners to admit Filipinos into their exclusive clubs, the scurrilous articles attacking the integrity of Filipinos, and the basic inequities in various treaties.

If foreigners have to be educated to respect the Filipino, Filipinos are only too willing to oblige. And it is to the credit of foreigners in this country that they read the handwriting on the wall, and peacefully give in.

The latest outrage that has come to our attention is the alleged racial discrimination in salary scales in foreign subsidiaries. We have been the recipient of information relating to the wage policies of one particular firm.

In this company, 22 foreign executives receive more (₱2,257,034.10) in annual salaries than 136 Filipino executives do (₱2,013,320). The average salary of a foreign executive is more than six times that of a Filipino.

The highest paid Filipino who holds the position of a vice president and member of the board of directors — a position that should be second only to the top — is paid a lower salary than the lowest paid of the 22 foreign executives.

The Filipino vice president receives ₱44,000 per annum. The lowest paid foreigner is an American who married a Filipina, a labor relations manager, and he receives ₱44,515. The second lowest paid foreigner is a Spaniard, a technical assistant to a department manager, receiving ₱62,570.07; the third lowest is an American who is not married to a Filipina, a manager of advertising, receiving ₱76,979.96. The highest paid foreigner who is the immediate boss of the Filipino vice president receives ₱163,-876.19.

The salary scale for foreigners, according to reports, is fantastically higher than those for Filipinos.

The Filipino vice president receives ₱44,000; his foreign counterpart receives ₱139,940.

Three Filipino department managers receive ₱32,400 (public relations), ₱22,128 (sales promotion), ₱22,644 (national accounts). Their foreign counterparts receive ₱112,-385 (general office), and ₱76,978 (advertising).

Three Filipino district managers receive ₱24,960, ₱21,-360 and ₱21,300 respectively. One foreign district manager receives ₱79,195; and a foreign assistant district manager receives ₱91,296.

A Filipino assistant to the department manager receives ₱22,044; his foreign counterpart receives ₱62,570.

Our immigration laws allow the entry of foreign personnel on "pre-arranged employment" based on the condition that no Filipino is qualified to take the job. There is no quarrel over the contention that foreigners may have to be paid a higher salary (overseas pay) to come on temporary basis and train Filipinos to take over the job.

But it must be remembered that foreigners are here to train Filipinos, not to displace them. When these foreigners take on the jobs *permanently* — then they must at least be subject to the same salary scale as Filipinos; otherwise it is rank discrimination.

Is it possible that no Filipino can be found to take over such fields as (1) marketing, (2) personnel administration, (3) accountancy, (4) advertising, (5) legal matters, (6) finance and (7) labor relations — as may be claimed by this particular company?

I had been in private business before, and it is no secret that a foreigner earning $7,200 (or ₱28,800) per annum abroad is paid about ₱60,000 to come here. In addition, he is given free use of a car, free housing, free transportation, club privileges and a practically unlimited expense account. He likes it here in the Philippines where he receives all in all three times what he receives back home, and enjoys a cost of living which is one-third what it is back home. His standard of living rises nine times; he can afford servants galore to do the dishes, the laundry and the baby sitting. He acquires a sense of importance in the community and the doors of elegant society open at his bidding. It is a great life.

And so, inevitably, confidential reports are sent back to the home office that no Filipino is competent enough to take his place.

When will Filipinos be ready to take over? The answer is when they are ready as the Negroes were in Southern United States, to fight for their rights in the courts, in the legislature, in peaceful demonstrations, over the bargaining table or before the bar of public opinion.

————O————

THE RICE AND FAULT OF THE
FILIPINO PEOPLE

The Rice and Fault of the Filipino People may be a puny pun on the Rise and Fall of the British Empire, but it may have a similar degree of impact upon the course of history.

For rice is the staple food of Asia's teeming millions, two thirds of the world's population, who are precariously close to the brink of starvation, full of wild hopes impossible of fulfillment, and poised ominously to inflict their presence on the rest of mankind. Not having enough rice may tilt this world into chaos and self-destruction.

For the Philippines, not having enough rice may mean a despondent dependence on those upon whom we dare not depend, loss of leadership in Southeast Asia, trouble within our own frontiers, and a breach in the ramparts of our freedoms.

Already the perennial problem of rice has beaten into sad shape the history, the economy, the psychology, and physiognomy of our people.

The problem of rice shortage has been our lot since 1910 when the Philippies became the chosen instrument of America's Manifest Destiny. Conditions were so created that it was as if the American colonial administrators said: "Don't produce what you need; produce instead what we want. We buy your sugar, and you use the money to buy the rice you need." By real design or not, it was a classic case of a colonial import-export economy.

Rice was imported to "stabilize prices," which actually meant making rice available to the people at the cheapest price possible. Thus the cheap rice policy was born. People bought rice at the corner store at cheap subsidized prices — but what they did not realize was that they actually paid for the full cost of the rice, since the price difference (subsidy) was paid out of the taxes they paid. Moreover, the subsidy was paid to foreign rice growers at the expense of Filipino producers who were discouraged from producing enough.

And so for the last 54 years, since 1910, the Philippines imported rice, every single year except during the war years and two lucky years (1960 and 1962). And for the last 54 years, through American Democratic and Republican administrations during the colonial period, through Nacionalista and Liberal party administrations during the Commonwealth and postwar periods, elections were won and lost, governments rose and fell with the fluctuations of the price of rice.

It was as if the people in a rare consensus say: "Mr. Government, give us cheap rice or else . . . you won't be around to do anything else!"

But economic development demands temporary sacrifices. And the people in effect rendered their mandate thus: "Yes, we are willing to pay the price for development. We are willing to pay a high price for cars, refrigerators, and TV sets. We are willing to pay a high price for cigarettes and subsidize the tobacco industry; we are willing to pay the political price of parity and compromised national dignity to help the traditional export industries. We are willing to pay for all these in order to industrialize our country, and provide hope for future generations. We will sacrifice on most things — but we will not sacrifice on the food we put on our children's mouths! We cannot postpone the consumption of food. We must eat today so that we may live to reap the benefits of tomorrow."

Since the Filipino people and the government do not have enough resources to pursue all-out development of all sectors, the direction of national efforts were concentrated in the agricultural export and manufacturing industries.

But the rice industry? Any national discussion of the situation is beclouded by a hysterical campaign of vilification carried on by a small group of caciques who alienate the sympathy of government leaders and the consuming public.

Every administration from Quezon to Macapagal has tried its best to insure that we shall never lack the one commodity essential to life and to our very existence as a nation. We have set up the International Rice Research Institute where rice technology has been developed to an extent achieved nowhere else in the world.

We have learned, and we have taught most other Asian nations (except ourselves, it seems) the techniques of improving rice yield (up to 250 cavanes per hectare), scientific seed selection (for rice that matures in amazinglv short period of 90 days), the use of herbicides to control weeds and insecticides to control pests, and many other ways of producing rice beyond our wildest dreams.

Our government is building irrigation systems (the most important single factor in rice production), selling fertilizer at half the cost (which had to be stopped because the rice farmer sells the fertilizer to the citrus and sugar farmers), making available selected seeds, and extending massive credit in the form of low interest loans to the rice farmers.

But it cannot provide the necessary motivation to produce because of the overwhelmingly unanimous and uncompromising demand of the Filipino people for cheap rice.

Because of the cheap rice policy, two generations of the Filipino people have acquired bad eating habits. We eat more rice than we should. We are overfed and undernourished. We eat an excess of carbohydrates, but little of the body-building proteins that we need.

The American fills his belly with steaks and beans — with only about three slices of bread for his carbohydrate needs. The Japanese eat herbs and fish without rice throughout his meal; a small cup of rice is presented later as some sort of dessert.

But the average Filipino fills his plate with a high mound of rice, and follows the advice of his grandmother (I'm sure most of our readers have experienced this) :

"Hijo, rice is the staff of life itself. Eat as much rice as you can. But eat as little of meat and other foods, because victuals and viands are expensive and are only there to make rice more palatable to eat. Eat rice, rice, and more rice."

What grandma does not know is that the excess volume of rice we eat goes down the drain of body excretion; that we deny ourselves enough meat and mongo beans to build our bodies to normal growth. The result is that we Filipinos are a small people — squat, slight, and bony, and in some cases all fat without muscles.

The rice problem is the fault of the Filipino people and may well prove to be the unvital link between the rise and fall of the Filipino people.

THE EMERGING MIDDLE CLASS

For 425 years, the white man lorded it over his little brown brother with the sword, the cross and the dollar sign. For 425 inbreeding, frustrating years, the Filipino tao was tied to the soil, a veritable feudal serf, under caciques and foreign colons who fattened themselves on the fruits of his labor.

The Philippines was forced into a colonial type of plantation economy, as a supplier of raw materials and a dumping ground for factory rejects and surplus products. Wealth became an exclusive merry-go-round affair within the vicious circle of landowners, importers and exporters — and the common tao looked in from the outside, hardly earning enough to keep body and soul together.

The common tao has been driven to work hard, from dawn to dusk, day in and day out — without any hope of earning any more than his father and forefathers before him. He has been made to see that wealth comes, not from calloused hands, but from itching palms and silver spoons; that the money that is forever wasted in an orgy of conspicuous consumption is often stolen or inherited, seldom earned by persistence and hard work. And so the common tao aspires through other means to achieve material success — marrying the landlord's daughter, winning sweepstakes, gambling, usury and politics.

The common tao cannot and does not concern himself with affairs beyond the problem of the next day's meal for his growing family. From this burden, he occasionally escapes to a dream world of fiestas and Bahala Na. He will vote for the man who makes the wildest political promises on the desperate hope that at least some of the promises will be kept; or for the man who offers him lechon, tuba, a handshake or a small loan to ease the tribulations of tomorrow; or for any man strong enough to command his blind, unreasoning and extremely personal loyalty.

Because of this, the politics of the Philippines have long been the happy hunting grounds of every sort of economic parasite — from opportunists to racketeers, from communists to carpetbaggers. And the common tao, locked in the daily struggle with hunger and high prices, is too tired to care.

But throughout the length and breadth of the land, this election year of 1965, is heard the clamor of many other voices — organized, insistent, demanding to be heard.

In almost every center of population, myriad organizations spring up like mushrooms — civic clubs, business chambers, trade unions and every conceivable association of persons willing to speak out collectively and effectively — from the Jaycees to the Rotarians, from the Philippine Chamber of Industries to the Lapiang Manggagawa, from the Committee for Good Government to the National Federation of Women's Clubs; from Iglesia ni Cristo to the Holy Name Society.

No government actuation, no legislative bill or law, or for that matter, no public or private act, has ever escaped the scathing scrutiny of their resolutions and petitions. Through the radio and newspapers, in every public hearing, in every picket line, they speak out with a boldness never before experienced in the public scene — striking fear into the hearts of caciques and carpetbaggers, and all the sacred sows and brazen idols who have always held our country in silent, strangulating grip.

They minded everybody's business, from collecting garbage to the Laurel-Langley Agreement. And a measure of their growing influence is the extent to which politicians vie for a chance to be invited as their guest speakers.

From all walks of life they come, but there is one characteristic they share: they are intellectually independent because, in a great degree, they are financially independent. And they are financially independent because, unlike the parasitic cacique and colon, unlike the apathetic tao, most of them developed a certain amount of self-reliance, initiative, resourcefulness and talent for organization.

The emergence of the middle class is the direct result of our belated Industrial Revolution and the frenzied economic activities that followed in its wake.

The core of the great middle class and indeed its very reason for being, is the industrialist-entrepreneur. Whether we like like or not, the irresistible force of sheer economic necessity has made the industrialist the man of today, tomorrow and the next exciting hundred years.

After 425 years, there is hope that between forces tending towards a government by the traditional exploiters (called Colonialism), and forces tending towards a government by the traditionally exploited (called Communism), there has at last emerged a militant, intelligent and vocal middle class composed of factory owners, industrial workers and professionals — whose existence will guarantee a government of free independent men, called Democracy.

—————0—————

THE HISTORICAL PATTERN OF GROWTH

Primitive peoples, like the Aetas, the red Indians and African natives earned their living by hunting and foraging. They were nomadic; and they moved from place to place, stalking animals and picking fruits from forest trees to satisfy their needs. There was then no such thing as the "sacred right of property" since like the Jesuits, they all shared the means of production.

Later, people began to settle down in communities and acquired a sense of property, taming the animals and fencing them in grazing pastures, and cultivating crops in their own farm plots. They needed somebody to protect their lands from brigands, and the feudal lords protected them right out of the ownership of their lands. Thus was born the feudal, colonial type of agricultural economy, which long flourished in the pastoral peace of caciques and colons.

Then came the Industrial Revolution. The Machine brought about a shift from agriculture to industry. Industrialization absorbed the surplus farm population and paved the way for farm mechanization. *Although agricultural output continued to rise in absolute terms, it ceased to be the greatest contributor to national income.* Manufacture and service industries took on greater significance and contributed the greater share of the national income.

This broad historical pattern of growth — from hunting to agriculture to industry — underlies the schematic views of economic history, of such men of diverse schools as Adam Smith, Thomas Jefferson, Alexander Hamilton, Lord Maynard Keynes, Veblen, Rostov, to mention a few. And it is recognized by all that "underdeveloped" economies are almost always still in the agricultural stage; and "highly developed" economies generate little of their income by agriculture.

The history of the American economy shows this pattern of growth. In 1840, more than 50 percent of its national income was generated by agriculture. In 1865 by the end of the Civil War, the share of agriculture dropped to 20 percent. In 1920 at the end of World War I, this was reduced further to 10 percent. And today in the United States, agriculture generates less than 5 percent of the entire national income.

In the Philippines, agriculture generates 33 percent of the national income; in India, about 50 percent.

In the United States, the part of the labor force devoted to agriculture is only 8 percent; in the Philippines, 54.9 percent; in Nepal, which is still a feudal country, 93 percent.

In New Zealand, a supposedly agricultural country with one of the highest per capita income in the world, only 17 percent of its labor force are engaged in agriculture, producing only 20 percent of the entire national income.

Other countries of the world arrange themselves more or less on this scale — so much so in fact that we can safely assume that any country which specializes in agriculture is a poor country. And a country which does not specialize in agriculture is a relatively rich country.

Is the Philippines following this pattern of growth, or is it as stagnant as it was during the American colonial rule?

Under American administration, we were kept in an agricultural economy under a free trade (and parity) arrangement with the United States, by which we supplied America with agricultural raw materials in exchange for the finished goods we imported. And the unfairness of it all was that America unilaterally imposed "quotas" on our major exports while supplying us their manufactured goods in volume and diversity, absolutely without restrictions. Thus we were tied down to a few-crop agricultural economy, unable to industrialize under the sheer weight of unfair American competition.

Thank God for our independence. In spite of the free trade and parity provisions of the Bell Trade Act and the Laurel-Langley Agreement which tended to perpetuate the status quo, we began to industrialize under our initiative.

And we progressed more in the few years of independence than in all of the 50 years of the American colonial administration plus all the centuries of Spanish subjugation.

The change is there to see.

In 1939 at the end of American colonial rule, the percentage of the labor force engaged in agriculture and primary occupations was a stunning 76.7 percent; in 1959, this *decreased tremendously* to 58.2 percent; in 1964, further down to 54.9 percent.

In the same period, the percentage of the labor force employed in manufacturing and other non-primary occupations *increased* even more dramatically from 17.8 percent in 1939, to 36.3 percent in 1959, and up to almost 40 percent in 1964.

The national income was less than ₱1 billion in 1938 at the end of the colonial era; it rose to ₱6.5 billion in 1951, then to ₱16.0 billion in 1964.

Of this income, the share contributed by agriculture *decreased tremendously* from 65.8 percent in 1938, down to 43.0 percent in 1951, and down further to 33.1 percent in 1964.

Industry, moreover, *increased* its contribution from 10.2 percent in 1938 at the end of the American colonial period, up to 10.9 percent in 1951, and up to almost 21.4 percent in 1964.

Clearly, we are on our way toward joining the community of modern industrial nations. Thus in the air of freedom and political independence, inspite of those who would turn the clock back to the pastoral peace of caciques and colons, we Filipinos begin to behold the radiance of economic liberty, progress and prosperity, in this our land of the morning.

THE PLOW AND THE TRACTOR

A few all-knowing know-it-all foreigners who prowl the cocktail circuit, even as they feverishly move in to dominate our commerce and industry, are busily exhorting us credulous natives to "go back to the soil" and improve our agriculture before industrializing our economy.

For several decades now since long before the war, we have indeed been prodded by such pious preachments to devote most of our resources and economic efforts towards "rural development", ever inspired by the vision of eventual farm mechanization as in the United States — with tractors and harvesters, threshers and combines to usher in the promised Utopia.

But Utopia never came. Beyond the pale of neon-lights and city prosperity, the Filipino farmer still plods his weary way with carabao and plow, no better off than his ancestors were hundreds of years ago.

Why so?

At all levels of development, the general rule is that the most efficient combination of resources in the production of any goods is one which uses little of the costly resources and much of the cheaper resources.

In our economy where wages are low and the use of machinery is expensive, most farm work will naturally tend to be done by cheap labor.

A tractor costs more to buy than a carabao and plow. A tractor uses expensive gasoline while a carabao eats free grass. The labor saved in using a tractor is not enough to compensate for the costs of using a tractor. The time saved does not usually provide additional opportunities for gainful employment. So why use a tractor at all?

Labor is cheap in the Philippines because our primitive agricultural economy does not provide job opportunities in pace with population growth. Our people multiply in a geometric progression, like tilapia on a diet of durian. But job opportunities do not increase commensurately, dependent as they are on the area to be cultivated which forever remains the same.

The Filipino farm laborers have nowhere else to go, no other alternative to pursue but to stay in the farm and offer his labor for nothing more than the privilege of making a meager living. His labor is worth some ₱40 a year, and it is cheaper to hire more of his kind than to buy a tractor.

On the other hand, industrialization is an economic activity that provides job opportunities in proportion to population growth. Industry begets other industries, as man and woman beget children. Industrial laborers moreover, have to acquire training and discipline; and working side by side under one roof, they can unite to bargain collectively and effectively. Thus an industrial worker can command much higher wages than a farm laborer can, about ₱6 a day or ₱1,800 a year.

But when does farm mechanization and an agricultural revolution really start?

The answer is when the process of urbanization and industrialization, as it did in the United States, reaches a point wherein each farm laborer has an alternative — when he can say to the landowner: "I can go to a factory anytime and earn ₱6 a day. You must pay me as much if you want me to work in the farm."

Then the landowner in turn faces two choices. He can stop being an absentee landowner and tend to the farm himself. Or he can hire the tenant farmer for as much as industry is willing to pay.

In either case, he has to buy a tractor and other mechanized equipment. For he cannot afford to pay ₱6 a day to a farmer who works only with a plow and a carabao. He must provide him with a machine, as factories do, to multiply his productivity to a point where it is economically feasible to pay him ₱6 a day.

And also, if the landowner elects to tend the farm himself, a tractor is all his lily-white milking hands can handle. The absentee landlord with his prosperous belly, his queridas and cadillacs will be relegated to the past; and he becomes instead a gentleman farmer in an industrialized society, as has happened in the United States.

Does this mean fewer farmers will grow less food?

In the United States, only 8% of the American labor force are engaged in agriculture and other primary occupations, and they grow enough food not only to feed the whole United States but the rest of the free world as well, and have enough left over to plow under, to store and to give away.

In the Philippines, 54.9% of our labor population stay in the farms where all we have to do is to flick a seed into the ground to make it grow — and we cannot even produce enough to feed ourselves.

Everytime a foreign expert tells us to stop industrializing and "go back to the soil", he probably means six feet underground. It may do us well to offer him the proposition of exchanging places with our tenant farmer — the foreigner behind the plow, and our farmer in the cool airconditioned comfort of an executive suite.

————0————

NEC IN THE VANGUARD

The statement came from a foreign chamber of commerce with the characteristically colorful language with which it usually passes judgment on the people whose hospitality it enjoys.

The time was 1958 and the object of its criticism was the National Economic Council under the chairmanship of the venerable ex-Senator Jose Locsin, then laying down the policies of economic nationalism.

The foreign chamber editorialized with the wrath of God Almighty:

"It passes all understanding how any Economic Council rightfully so-called, could render such uneconomic counsel . . . . . nothing less than insane, threatening not simply injury and damage, but measureless loss and waste, retrogression and demoralization . . . . . systematic stifling, stunting and dwarfing . . . What sort of National Economic Council do we have which comes out with such maniacal proposals, which so completely subvert and negate . . .? This country's economic stability and progress . . . are menaced by, of all institutions, the National Economic Council."

Yet it may be said that were it not for the policy and planning of the National Economic Council, the Philippines might have developed into something like pre-war Shanghai or pre-Castro Cuba — dominated by feudal overlords and a parasitic class of foreign adventurers, gambler types and colonial traders — an intolerable situation that would have called for (it almost did!) a Mao-Tse-Tung or a Fidel Castro.

The National Economic Council under the chairmanship of such stalwarts as Manuel A. Roxas (destined to be the first president of our third republic), Miguel Cuaderno, Filemon Rodriguez, Alfredo Montelibano, Jose Locsin, Gil Puyat, Cornelio Balmaceda and Sixto Roxas, has consistently followed the course of *industrialization* and *economic nationalism* in an effort to change our feudal import-export plantation economy into a modern industrial one, characterized by the growth of a Filipino middle class of entrepreneurs, factory workers and professionals.

Contrary to popular impression, the National Economic Council — while its chairman is an extension of the power of the President as the highest paid cabinet member — is a legal body virtually independent of the executive department. Its membership consists of 3 Senators, 3 Congressmen, 3 members from the private sector and only 3 ex-officio members of the executive department. Provision has been made for minority party representation in the body.

By accident or design, the NEC membership always had a nationalistic orientation, as may be gleaned from the present membership: Senators Lorenzo Tañada, Gil Puyat, Ambrosio Padilla; Congressmen Rogaciano Mercado, Ramon Bagatsing, Ramon Durano; Labor leader Cipriano Cid, Economist Augusto Cesar Espiritu, Senior citizen Eugenio Padua, Commerce Secretary Cornelio Balmaceda, Central Bank Governor Andres Castillo, and Development Bank Chairman Pablo Lorenzo.

The NEC is the highest economic policy-formulating body in the Philippines and because of its bi-partisan, non-political membership embracing the legislative, executive and private sector, is in the best position to crystallize a national consensus on economic policy. It has been remarkably consistent and to the extent that its policies were implemented, so remarkably successful that the Philippines progressed more in 19 years under its own initiative than in all the 425 colonial years under American and Spanish masters.

Our overall trade had grown from $34 million in 1899 at the end of the Spanish era to $251 million in 1940 at the end of the American colonial period, to a staggering $1,413 million in 1964.

In 1939, our national income was only ₱1.03 billion still mostly in the hands of caciques and colons, with the common tao not earning much more than he did during the Spanish times; our per capita income was then ₱80 per year. In 1964 our national income was ₱16 billion better distributed among Filipinos; per capita income rose to ₱512 per annum.

In 1939, 75.9 per cent of the labor force was engaged in agriculture and other primary occupations; in 1964 the percentage went down to 54.8 per cent. From 1946 to 1964, the share of agriculture of the national income dipped from 45.4 per cent down to 33.1 per cent; the share of manufacturing jumped from 4.8 per cent up to 19.5 per cent. Clearly, in spite of caciques and foreign colons who advocate a "pastoral economy" the country is experiencing an industrial revolution.

Just before the war, a foreign chamber of commerce plotted against our independence saying in a printed pamphlet: "We are here by right, we are here by conquest and we have a title by conquest and a title by purchase. We are here as possessors and we are here as sovereigns; we are here as owners and controllers of absolute sovereignty."

It was the time when American investments, mostly domestic savings and reinvested domestic profits rather than new capital, totalled 73 per cent of all investments in public utilities, 37 per cent of mining, 36 per cent of the sugar industry, 21 per cent of commercial establishments, 46 per cent of coconut mills, 36 per cent of forestry.

Today although American investments have increased several times fold, their share of total investments as per the latest tax census is *only 1.2 per cent*. And majority of the American investors are of the new breed of liberal-minded democratic Americans who have the utmost respect for their Filipino hosts, who come in joint ventures with Filipino citizens, never treat us like Negroes or red Indians, do not muscle in to destroy Filipino businesses, and certainly do not intrude upon centers of political power with offensive familiarity.

And for all these, we should thank the National Economic Council under the chairmanship of President Manuel A. Roxas all the way down to the present leadership.

————O————

COTTAGE INDUSTRIES

From President Quezon's Social Justice Program to President Roxas' Bagong Katipunan, from President Quirino's total economic mobilization program to President Garcia's Filipino First Policy — common sense dictated that small-scale cottage industries are the foundation of any movement to free the Filipino "tao" from his ancient bondage. Yet all these years till President Macapagal created the NACIDA, lip service was all that was offered where action was the need.

As a result, cottage industries became synonymous with the making of clay pots, the weaving of buri hats, and the carving of little wooden souvenirs.

We need a cottage industry similar to that of Japan, a class of small entrepreneurs engaged, not in handicraft, but in industrial production using modern methods to produce in commercial quantities, not souvenirs, but articles of common use.

Cottage industries in Japan, by their very nature, are economically engaged in labor-intensive processing and assembly work. They make fountain pens, chinaware, metal art work, candies, furniture, plastic products, toys and novelties. They do preliminary processing in the pencil industry and others. They do final assembly work in the radio and electronic industries. They are part and parcel of the whole industries set-up of Japan; they are an important cog in the Japanese economy.

What are cottage industries in the Philippines? Are they anything more than useless appendages to the barrio's subsistence economy, part of the plantation type of feudal existence? Hat weaving and pot making — such are the manifestations of age-old primitive production, and they have little place in a modern industrial nation.

107

Cottage industries are the bridge between the old feudal order and full-scale industrialization for several reasons.

Firstly, cottage industries provide the opportunity to train the greatest number of people in the fine art of entrepreneurship; to develop their talent for organization, production, and marketing; to initiate them into the disciplines and attitudes of an industrialized society.

Take a farmer out of a farm and into a factory and he is a fish out of water. The farmer is used to working alone, physically apart from other farmers, each assigned his own separate plot of land to cultivate. Take this farmer and tell him to work with industrial laborers, rub shoulders with them under conditions of teamwork and cooperation, and he is lost. He is not used to teamwork. He is not used to group responsibility and discipline.

The farmer is used to working only three months out of every year, between harvest and planting time. His time is his own in the farm, he does not have to keep strict hours by the clock. Put this farmer in a factory, tell him he must work 8 full hours a day, day by day for 300 days a year, and he is lost. That is not the way he works in the slow and easy pace of farm life.

The farmer is paid by the crop he raises. His success or failure depends mostly on the weather which is outside his control. Tell him he shall be paid by the time he spends working; tell him he is subject to the orders of a foreman; tell him his success or failure depends, not on the weather, but on his own skill, initiative, resourcefulness, and sense of responsibility; tell the farmer all these and you are asking him to be another person, to change his whole outlook and way of life.

Cottage Industries are the one effective way of introducing this farmer into the industrial society we want to build. It is the one effective way, not only to change his cultural pattern, but also to encourage him to master the intricacies of entrepreneurship . . . develop the talent for organization, calculate risks, and learn the techniques of raising capital, marketing, and the training of management and production skills.

Cottage industries do more than reorient the common tao to the demands of modern society; they are the first step towards full scale industrialization for yet another reason. They are the fastest and most effective way to channel idle personal savings into the productive endeavor. It is a fact that most of the money printed find their way out of circulation into bamboo tubes and coconut shells. The thrifty provincial folk are inclined to look askance at putting their money in the bank for others to use; indeed the 300 rural banks now in existence are not even enough to cover the requirements of the country. This tremendous amount of legal currency diverted out of the money and credit system has stultified our efforts to promote a rising level of investment in this country.

Cottage Industries provide the opportunity not only to lure out this idle capital but also to channel it towards productive endeavor. Potentially, the amount of capital that may be raised by small entrepreneurs in this country is much larger in the aggregate than the large capital presently employed by large industrial firms. In other words, the total amount raised by small capitalists is potentially greater than what few big capitalists are capable of raising.

THE CONSUMER AS FINAL JUDGE

It is said that the management of an enterprise is chiefly concerned about reconciling the demands of the irreconcilable — the demand for higher wages by the laborer, more dividends by the investor, more taxes by the government and lower prices by the consumer.

The management's dilemma is complicated even more by the non-monetary demands of these four.

In addition to higher wages, the laborer wants security of tenure, opportunities for advancement, and shorter hours of work (so he may have the time to enjoy the fruits of his labor).

In addition to more dividends, the investor wants liquidity and security of his investment.

In addition to more taxes, the government wants to be sure that the enterprise contributes to the nation's economic development.

In addition to lower prices of the goods he buys, the consumer wants continuity of supply and the highest quality attainable at the price he is willing to pay.

Of these four interacting forces, the first three have the more direct means to press their demands: the laborer, through collective bargaining; the investor, through the stockholders' meeting; and the government, through the coercive power of our laws.

But the consumer has no such direct means. From the viewpoint of the businessman, especially the big industrialist, the ultimate consuming public is a vague, indeterminate and unidentifiable mass of people with whom he must deal through the intermediation of distributors, wholesalers and retailers, and with whom he communicates through the newspapers, radio, TV and other mass media.

110

What industrialists almost forgot especially during the days when dollar allocations guaranteed a market, and what some industrialists keep forgetting even now, is that the business enterprise exists *primarily* to satisfy the demands of the consumer; and that the success or failure of the enterprise depends *ultimately* on its ability to satisfy such demands.

Laborers, investors and the government have a certain amount of vested interest in a specific firm; and company relations with such three are somewhat in the nature of a forced marriage. Consumer relations on the other hand, is a perpetual courtship, for the consumers owe no loyalty to the firm. For a few centavos price difference, consumers may switch to another brand. No ultimatum is given, no notice served, no demands presented, just the quiet and awesome verdict of capricious whimsical creatures sitting in anonymous, unanimous judgment. To many a firm, such is the Last Judgment.

Consumer relations, long neglected during the Import Controls, present the most pressing challenge to foreign subsidiaries and Filipino businessmen and industrialists today . . . to improve efficiency of production and quality control so as to insure the highest quality of goods at the price the consumer is willing to pay . . . to use all available tools of market research to discover what the consumer really need and want; to employ the most effective marketing techniques so as to create a mass market and achieve the economies of mass production . . . above all to discard such vicious conventionalities as collusion in bids, price fixing, cartelization of markets, price-cutting, trade mark piracy, bribery of purchasing agents, under-the-table rebates, stock manipulation, cornering of supply, and other such practices that come under "combinations and conspiracies in restraint of trade."

Such unfair trade practices are altogether too prevalent today, as they were during the formative period of the United States of America. The businessman should read history and profit from the lessons of the past —

unless he wants to see the inevitable rise of muckrakers and government intervention in the form of price control and anti-trust legislations.

CONSCIENCE OF THE BUSINESSMAN

At the time of our greatest advance in economic growth, the businessman who considers himself the vanguard of such progress, often feels that he is not being appreciated enough. Indeed he feels hurt when he finds that in the minds of the people, the businessman is not necessarily an inspiring national leader whose integrity is unquestioned and whose work is assumed to be unequivocably for the public good. A lot of this prejudice is based on the fact that the people believe, not always without foundation, that the businessman will put profit before everything else, even before the well-being of the community. This belief breeds acrimony, distrust and class hatred, and a feeling that industrialization is somehow a conspiracy against the rest of the population.

For this, the businessman has only himself to blame. For it cannot be denied that many of those who have pioneered in industry and created new wealth that should been used to create still more wealth, have succumbed to the forces of reaction and reverted back to the old forms of privilege, such as investment in land and conspicuous consumption, instead of persisting in the more adventurous ways of industrial investment to further widen the economic base of our society.

A few years ago, a group of TV assemblers proposed to raise the tariff duties on imported sets, in the name of industrialization and added job opportunities for our people. As a result, inspite of the protests of importers speaking against monopoly and high prices in behalf of the consumers, the duties on TV sets were raised to 150% ad valorem. Recently a petition was made by one manufacturer to raise the tariff on TV tubes, on the grounds that TV tube manufacture will advance further the process of industrialization. Such petition was vigorously opposed by the TV assemblers. What moral justification was there

113

for such an opposition? The arguments advanced by TV assemblers against TV tube manufacture were the very same ones advanced by importers against TV assembly. The arguments that TV assemblers now oppose, are the very same ones they raised against the importers. For TV assemblers, the process of industrialization ends where their self-interest begins — in the assembly of imported components and in local cabinet carpentry.

I have witnessed many such backtracking of principle by many other industrial groups seeking tariff protection for themselves while denying it to others — paint manufacturers fighting resin manufacturers, resin manufacturers fighting soya-bean oil processors, soya-bean oil processors fighting soy bean farmers. And recently, canning plants against tin plate manufacturers; and tin plate and galvanizing plants against the rolling mills.

Are the entrepreneurial groups still socially irresponsible? Are there no Adam Smiths, no Disraelis, to mold the conscience of this emerging class?

CHALLENGE TO THE ENTREPRENEUR

The Filipino people have chosen to bear temporary sacrifices to advance the great cause of industrialization. They are paying the high price of tariff protection to insure entrepreneurial profits for continued industrial expansion and increased job opportunities.

I do not think they deserve the kind of spectacle they are sometimes made to witness — the newly rich industrialists wallowing in the luxury of imported goods, while the rest of the population are forced to buy local products; the newly rich industrialists using their profits not to set up new enterprises but to travel abroad for pleasure, to set up mansions in Forbes Park, to invest in idle land for speculative purposes, to turn their wealth into jewels and conspicuous consumption. Are our entrepreneurs abandoning their task of capital formation, to join the ranks of the landed aristocracy and the idle rich?

To be sure, not all industrialists are of such bent. But the signs are disconcerting: While industrial stocks are selling at 60% of their actual value, land prices continue to climb to ridiculous heights. A foreign investor once told me how shocked he was to discover the price of industrial sites around Manila. At ₱30 per square meter, the price is equivalent to $30,500 per acre. The price of industrial sites in New York State, complete with roads, power, water and sewage, comes up to one third of the local price, only $10,000 per acre. In South America, where the foreign investor recently set up a plant, he paid less than one-tenth of the local price — $2,000 per acre. Even residential land is expensive. A lot in Bel-Aire that was offered for ₱43 per square meter two years ago now sells for ₱135 per square meter.

On the other hand, the common stocks of some of the new industrial and commercial ventures are selling in the stock market thus: Celulosa, par of ₱10, sells at ₱7.80 per share; DRB Marketing, par of ₱1.00, bid price of ₱0.82 per share; Ramie Textiles, par of ₱1.00, asking price of ₱0.38; Universal Cement, par of ₱1.00, bid price of ₱0.52 per share.

Is risk capital gravitating from industrial ventures back into the traditional form of land speculation? If so, the industrialist faces a new challenge to revive the flagging spirit of entrepreneurship and rededicate himself to industrialization and real capital formation.

If capital formation has not reached the level of self-sustaining growth, it is probably because most of our entrepreneurs are still self-centered and family oriented in their financial attitudes. Most of our industries are organized as sole proprietorships or as closed family corporations with small risk capital and heavy borrowings, their expansion woefully limited to reinvestment of profits. Mergers and consolidations that may lead to more efficient units of production, are at once rejected because of sheer personal and family pride. The operation of such industries are stubbornly held by members of the family regardless of ability or lack of it.

I maintain that the industrialist-entrepreneur, upon whom the nation rests its hopes for economic advancement, has a higher duty and responsibility than mere personal accumulation of wealth; he has to respond to the challenge of stimulating the participation of the rest of the Filipino people into the grand adventure of entrepreneurial risk taking; of subordinating his personal empire building to the needs for efficient and effective production units, to help create a professional managerial class without which no nation can hope to achieve a self-sustaining rate of economic advancement.

OUR POTENTIAL EXPORT TRADE

Probably the greatest challenge that faces the industrialist and businessman of the Philippines lies in the field of export trade. With a higher foreign exchange rate, and with labor costs adjusted down to lower than that of Hongkong, there is a decided incentive in this direction. In the great diversity of goods that industry today produces for the local market, and in the variety of skills that were given opportunity to flourish, surely our industrialists have found the skills to make certain products better and cheaper than the rest of the world can. When we export, not the traditional raw materials, but the products of our industrial skills, then the Philippines can truly move into the society of industrialized nations.

But the Philippines will enter the arena of world trade at an extreme disadvantage, for it must compete with aggressive and fully industrialized nations such as Germany, Japan and the United States. The various regional economic blocs that have come into being these last few years, such as the European Economic Community and the Outer Seven, are now in a position not only to dictate the price at which we can sell our traditional raw materials, but also to keep our finished goods at a tariff disadvantage. The point I am leading to is this: Instead of trying to compete with well-established nations in already developed international markets, why do we not explore new trade routes and develop new markets for ourselves? Here the answer lies much closer than we think — in the developing markets of Southeast Asia.

Filipino businessmen have built hotels in Hongkong, opened up insurance companies in Malaya, made movies in Indonesia — why not export our finished goods and technical knowhow? One Filipino industrialist is negotiating a joint venture with his knowhow as his contributed capital, for the manufacture of paint in Thailand, and the manufacture of resins in Malaya. There is a wealth of export possibilities to Indonesia for wheat flour, textiles, cement, fertilizers, appliances, cars and other consumer goods. Filipino businessmen should explore these export possibilities, even if they have to sell at cost in order to invade the market.

For soon, sooner than we expect, an Asian Common Market will come into being — perhaps on a sub-regional basis to begin with, among the ASA countries and Indonesia. In such a market of some 170 million consumers will our true mettle be tested — with all the natural resources at our command necessary for all-out industrialization, with the mass market needed to support vast industries at optimum capacity of operation, and with all historic mission of ushering our country out of the status of a banana republic into the community of modern industrialized nations of the world.

————0————

RIZAL'S "PROSPEROUS ENGLAND"

Dr. Jose Rizal, in his novel "El Filibusterismo", in unveiling his dream of the future of the Philippines, wrote:

"Tomorrow . . . . commerce, industry, agriculture, the sciences will develop under the mantle of liberty, with wise and just laws, as in prosperous England."

"Prosperous England," Rizal said, and elsewhere in his novel, he said through Simoun the jeweler, "Study how other nations prosper. And do as they did."

Prosperous England, at the time of young Rizal, was a "nation of shopkeepers" that brought Napoleon to his knees, wrought the world's first Industrial Revolution and emerged as the greatest nation on the face of the earth, mistress of all the seas, and lord of lands upon which the sun never set.

Yet there was a time when England was in the Middle Ages what the Philippines is today — a country where "laziness is a vice" as the English author, Inge, once wrote — an exporter of raw materials and an importer of finished goods.

England in the Middle Ages derived its sole income from the exports of raw wool, as we derive our income from sugar and copra. The wool was processed by the Flemish weavers in Belgium and imported back into England as woolen cloth.

The first decisive step was taken in the reign of Edward IV who banned the exportation of wool and imposed heavy duties on the importation of woolen cloth. Thus the English were forced by royal edict to utilize their wool to make their own woolen cloth. The Flemish went out of business, and England became the world's leading exporter of woolen products. The English became proficient in

119

spinning and weaving and expanded into linen, silk and cotton.

Exactly the same policy of prohibition and protection was employed to foster the iron industry. As early as the days of Edward III, the export of iron was forbidden. Edward IV absolutely prohibited the importation of iron goods, which up to his time, was supplied by Germany.

From the primary industries of textile and iron, the Industrial Revolution came into being. Each industry created other industries; each industry provided capital, labor, skill, technology, and a market for more industries. The demand for spinning and weaving machinery created the first machine tool industry; the need for pumps to keep water out of the coal mines created the steam-engine; the need to transport coal led to the invention of the locomotive.

It was not by half-way measures that England achieved greatness. When a new industry secured its position in the home market, an export subsidy assured capture of the world market. The Navigation Acts were imposed to secure world supremacy at sea, and paved the way for the acquisition of colonies to ensure an expanding market and a source of materials.

Thus England's rise of greatness was not due to some "innate quality of her people," according to L. S. Emery, but "the result of *deliberate statecraft* devoted over the centuries to the development of wealth-building industries and the creation of ever new and varied aptitudes in her people." This deliberate statecraft was the strong protectionist policy pursued by the English government up to the year 1845.

Study "prosperous England", and do what she did, Rizal said.

America, Germany and Japan followed Rizal's advice. By rigorous tariff protection, they built their mighty industrial empires.

120

It is interesting to note that England, confident in its role as an industrial colossus among backward nations, became a free trader in 1845 and flourished on its Empire trade. In the meantime, it was fighting a losing battle against the protectionist policies of Germany, America, Japan and other countries. In 1931, England finally abandoned its free trade policy. It is now America's turn to advocate free trade.

It is also interesting to note that the economic colonial policy of England for its 13 colonies in America caused the War of Independence; and that English economic experts for many years after the Civil War were "still lecturing Americans about the mistake they were making in protecting their industries."

History repeats itself, and we have America implanting the same colonial policy in the Philippines and even now, long after our independence, American experts are lecturing us about the mistake of protecting our infant industries.

Even now American experts are telling us to concentrate on "rural improvement" to seduce us away from industrialization, back to the pastoral peace of a plantation economy. They say "concentrate on export industries" to make sure we continue to be raw material exporters. They clamor for "free enterprise" to perpetuate foreign domination of our economy. They decry "high tariffs" as a barrier to "free trade."

And fools that we are, we forget Rizal's advice.

He said: Do what England and America did.

By no stretch of imagination did he say: Do as Americans tell you to do.

————O————

THE TRAGEDY OF OUR PAST

Five hundred years ago, before the Spaniards came, we had a primitive but ideal economic setup. Each community was economically independent, producing for its own needs and wants. There was full employment for each man tilled his own farm and operated a small home industry to supply his tools, clothing and shelter. Supply and demand were in perpetual balance, because buyers and suppliers were in constant physical contact and the demand rarely varied from a few basic necessities.

Left to ourselves, we might have been able, as Japan did, to modernize our economy, urbanize, industrialize and create a viable economic unit, not of one community, but of a whole nation.

But history was against us.

When the Spaniards came, they took away from us our lands and our freedom. The fruits of our labor were seized by encomienderos who wasted our wealth in conspicuous consumption or brought it back to Spain with them. For the next four hundred years, the mass of our people lived from hand to mouth, with no accumulated savings to increase their capacity to buy or capacity to produce.

The Americans came, and with them the surplus products of their highly developed factories. The influx of these mass produced goods, by sheer weight of unfair competition, incapacitated what was left of our infant industries. Worse than that, the economy of the Philippines was tied down to a few export crops — raw materials for America's factories. Agriculture became specialized, but not mechanized. Because there were no industries to absorb excess agricultural labor, the fields were tilled by hand and the farmers were ill-paid. The benefits of modern technology were available only to the rich land-owning class who, by the grace of the Paris Treaty, were allowed to keep their royal grants.

The Japanese came and isolated us from the rest of the world, then proceeded to rob us of our wealth. To our surprise we never really starved. The farmer increased his income and capacity to buy because few landowners dared to go to the provinces to collect their rental dues. Without foreign competition, our infant industries thrived — comparatively inefficient perhaps due to our inexperience but productive enough to support ourselves and the Japanese invaders. Inspite of the hardships of the times — lack of medicines, induced inflation, blood bath on the hills — there was a glimmer of confidence that, left to our own resources and without the burden of Japanese occupation, the Filipino people can with a little self-sacrifice achieve the status of an industrialized nation.

Liberation came and with it the total destruction of most of our tangible assets. We were destitute and demoralized and we looked to American for succor.

Independence came and America came across with a helping hand, but not without strings. The American people were quite willing to help the common tao up to $1,000 worth of war damage payments. As for the rich people who lost a good deal more, there was a price to pay and the price was the Bell Trade Act. The land-owning class was assured a temporary preferential status in the American market for various export products such as sugar, copra, and hemp; and war damage payments over $1,000 were to be paid — on these conditions: (1) American finished products will be allowed to enter the Philippines duty-free; (2) we must change our Constitution to allow Americans to exploit our natural resources on the same basis as the Filipinos.

It was strictly a business proposition which the entire Filipino people through a plebiscite had the power to accept or reject. The entire country split into two camps — but on the wrong issue. The opponents of the Act took their stand against the parity provision. The paramount issue on whether duty-free American products would destroy our budding industries, was obscured and forgotten in the dust and confusion of battle. One of the few who realized the true implications of the Bell Trade Act was Salvador Araneta who deserves special mention here. "Prophet of disaster" he was called and his voice was a cry in the wilderness. And the proponents of the Act skillfully maneuvered the issue into National Pride vs. Starvation.

The Bell Trade Act was of course accepted, and the Philippines directed its economic efforts towards the production of raw materials for export rather than on the production of goods for domestic consumption. It was a reactionary move, a costly mistake.

The American bonanza that came in the form of war damage and rehabilitation payments, surplus equipment and United States army expenditures, was mostly used up in an orgy of insatiable consumption of duty-free American goods which flooded the country and totally obliterated our infant industries. A little of that bonanza was diverted towards the rehabilitation of our pre-war export industries — but what good did it do? The world market for copra was poor, because of the development of chemical detergents and the unacceptable quality of our production. The artificially created market for sugar in the States stood in danger of competition from Cuba and Hawaii which are closer to America. Hemp suffered from the mosaic disease and the competition of nylon and South American hemp.

Within the national economy the main flow of wealth passed from the hands of the absentee landowner in the form of export products, through the exporters out of the country; and then came back as finished products through the importers and back to the landowners. Wealth was a merry-go-round affair within the exclusive circle of landowners, exporters — and the common tao looked in from the outside, hardly earning any more than he did during the Spanish times.

The Import Control came suddenly with the stark realization that our export industries do not earn enough dollars to enable us to import even our basic necessities. The landowners - importer - exporter group secured high priority for dollar-earning industries and hopefully predicted the end of import controls as soon as more dollars are earned. The tempting vision of American goods fresh from modern factories flowing into the Philippines for the enjoyment of all, was held up to the Filipino people to anticipate and drool over, to hope and pray for.

Into the scene has come a new and dynamic group of industrialists. Most of them started as home industries and gradually grew into industrial complexes such as Puyat and Teodoro. Some came from the landowner-exporter-importer group, but entered the field of industry with a mission, such as Soriano, Elizalde and Araneta. Some came from abroad, bringing with them the wisdom and economic drive of their more advanced countries such as PMC and Caltex. With the advent of Import Control and elimination of foreign competition, these industrialists have grown in size, number and influence. This new industrial middle-class, composed of financially and intellectually independent factory owners who regard themselves as harbingers of a belated Industrial Revolution has challenged the 400-year-old economic supremacy of feudal overloads.

"At every crossing on the road that leads to the future, every progressive spirit is opposed by a thousand men appointed to guard the past" according to Maeterlinck.

In today's era of decontrol — two forces now stand at the crossroads of our destiny: one committed to the perpetuation of the status quo, the other, to the challenge of an exciting future.

THE TURNING POINT

Before the war, the Philippines had an economy based on what was fondly called "free enterprise." Actually it was not any more free than it is now. The whole economic system was geared to make the Philippines an economic dependency of the United States. The tariff structure was set to encourage importation of finished goods and exportation of raw materials. Free trade provisions kept this country an exclusive preserve for American businessmen and excluded fair competition from Japanese and European suppliers. While America was allowed to export any and all kinds of goods to the Philippines without restriction, the Philippines was not allowed to compete freely with American goods in the United States which imposed quantitative restrictions on each of our major exports. .

In spite of these lopsided restrictions, we had a comparatively favorable balance of trade with the United States. But it became increasingly clear that time was against us. We developed a plantation type of economy comparable to that of banana republics in South America, with no domestic industries to speak of; with the monetary sector of our economy confined to the vicious circle of landlords, exporters, and importers; with the rest of our population existing at subsistence levels with no opportunities to trade save by simple barter. We were forced to trade our raw materials, which are irreplaceable, with the products of American skills, which are not only cumulative but also self-perpetuating. And while our consumption imports rose with our growing population, our exports were kept within limits of the quota imposed by the United States. We were destined for the poorhouse and we did not know it.

It was only a question of time before we realized that our type of feudal, agricultural economy could never keep up with our population growth.

126

The Second World War hastened this process of economic deterioration. With our export industries destroyed, and with the pent-up demand for consumption goods after the war, our imports exceeded our exports year by year at an alarming rate. It did not take long before the country's trade deficit became so great that our foreign exchange reserve was forced down to an alarming low level. By 1949, bold and drastic measures had to be instituted to save the country from bankruptcy.

Import and exchange controls were thus imposed on the Philippine economy. Whatever else may be said about the economic controls, there is no question but that at the time they were instituted, they were badly needed emergency measures not only to check the unnecessary demand for imports, but also to pursue the industrialization program to which the government was committed.

The decade of the 1950's, the era of import and exchange controls, will probably be judged by future historians as the turning point of this nation's economy. During this decade, there was a decided shift in direction from an export economy to a more diversified production for domestic consumption, from agricultural and tribal ways of living to industrial employment, from consumption to production. During this decade, the national income rose by 61 per cent, and the manufacturing sector's share of this income rose by an unbelievable 178 per cent. As a result the per capita income of the Filipino people became the 3rd largest in the Eastern Hemisphere, being surpassed only by Japan and by Malaya.

But the most important legacy of the controls is the emergence of the industrial middle class — bold, young entrepreneurs of finance and industry, men of initiative and imagination, who brought this nation to the take-off stage of industrialization.

In spite of the country's industrial gains, however, with the increasing officiousness of the bureaucratic machinery, many people tended to be more and more critical of controls. Inherent in the idea of controls is the rationing of scarce foreign exchange and a selective system to discriminate as to who should use them and for what purpose. As such, therefore, susceptibility to favoritism and graft was a built-in feature of the system.

An increasing number of industrialists and entrepreneurs became more dissatisfied with the administration of controls, especially when it tended to prejudice the establishment of new industries and preserve the new status quo. The Central Bank could no longer give dollar support to the fast-growing entrepreneurial class. And those who could not establish or expand their industries demanded a return to free competition.

Critics called attention to the fact that controls are inherently emergency measures only and were never meant to be permanent fixtures in the economy. The major point of contention, therefore, during the last few years was not whether controls were desirable, but whether the time for lifting them had already come.

And the time came for decontrol. What change did controls effect in our economy?

In 1949, our pre-war industries were still in the stage of rehabilitation; in 1960, not only do we have a much greater and much more diversified export potential but we have also established a wide range of domestic industries producing for local consumption. In 1949, our adult population still largely consisted of farmers, bureaucrats and veterans working for handouts; in 1960, we have a new and well-organized industrial labor force, and a dynamic class of entrepreneurs fully exploiting the fields of industry, finance and marketing. In 1949, we had practically no banking system outside of Manila, in 1960 we have 20 commercial banks and some 140 rural banks all over the islands. By 1960, we have seen the growth of public corporations, investment and finance companies on a scale we never dreamed of in 1949.

The controls set a new direction to our economy and set it on the road to industrialization. And the new challenges the Decontrol poses, promise that the best is yet to come.

THE INDUSTRIALIST AND THE FEUDALIST

The landed aristocracy and its ally, the class of foreign colonial traders (let's call them "Feudalists" for lack of a better term) whose interests lie in the perpetuation of a feudal economy, seem formidable. For centuries, they have accumulated wealth, prestige, and influence.

Come now the industrialist and his ally — the burgeoning middle class of professionals and factory workers — with a bid to win the support of the masses. Their wealth increases at a geometric rate, as can only happen in the field of industry.

Point by point, on basic principles, the industrialist takes issue with the feudalist.

The feudalist solemnly demands that priority be given to dollar-earners. The industrialist argues that if this country is to be self-sufficient, we should direct our energies toward producing finished goods for our own consumption. Therefore it is more important to reduce the need for spending dollars than it is to earn more dollars to spend. In other words, priority must be given to dollar-saving industries which produce our basic necessities and wants.

The feudalist says that no industry must be allowed which does not use local materials. The industrialist agrees partly, but argues that it is more desirable to import foreign raw materials than foreign finished products. The industrialist further contends that more important than the use of our material resources is the development of our labor resources. Our material wealth may lie under the earth, awaiting the day it can be economically developed. But the labor value of an idle day is lost forever. And it is imperative for us to make use of the labor of our untold number of unemployed, even if we initially buy our raw materials from abroad.

"But if we don't have export industries, where will you get the dollars to buy the raw materials?" challenges the feudalist. To which the industrialist counters: "We do not intend to eliminate export industries entirely. We only mean to relegate them to a subordinate role — which is to provide the dollars for the importation of capital equipment and raw materials (certainly not finished goods). Eventually, with consistent government support and the development of full scale industries, we will be able to (1) exploit Philippine raw materials economically, and (2) export finished goods (not raw materials) abroad to pay for the materials we do not have — just like Japan, England and America. Then the feudalist will depend less on the exportation of sugar, copra and hemp; and concentrate more on rice, cotton, poultry and dairy products for the Filipino people. We will absorb their tenants into our factories, so they will be forced to mechanize and lower their costs!"

But 400 years of economic prosperity have developed his resistance to change and the feudalist takes refuge in the argument that belies a colonial mentality. "But the Filipino consumer prefers American goods that you cannot deny!"

This is about the last straw for the industrialist. The blood of Lapu-Lapu rises from the depths of his ancestry and he cries out: "Four centuries of foreign domination, four centuries of economic servitude with no hope for advancement, has led the poor Filipino to believe in dreams and Bahala, in winning sweepstakes and marrying the landlord's daughter, in Santa Claus and political promises! The poor Filipino will splurge his paycheck on a pack of Salem cigarettes — then spend the rest of the month displaying the Salem package with local cigarettes inside, with a comical pride that is all too tragic to laugh at. Sure he prefers American cars and refrigerators, as much as he believes in fairy tales — because the poor Filipino can never afford to buy them, and would like to have them around for a kind of wistful window-shopping spree."

The feudalist in a pacifying tone, now brings up the matter of confidence in the Filipino's industrial skill:

"Well, before we allow him to start an industry, he must prove that he can make as good and as cheap a product as those imported." The industrialist accepts the challenge with few reservations: "You try to force us to utilize still undeveloped sources of raw materials — and then expect us to compete successfully with industrialized America, where a thousand firms work on the product from raw materials to finished form. Oh no! Limit the importation of finished goods through tariffs, just as they did in Japan, England, and America during their formative years. Give us the time to develop our technical skills and overcome consumer prejudice without the added burden of foreign competition. Then watch competition among local firms boost the quality and lower the price of our products."

The feudalist attacks a sore point, "Ah, but you industrialists exploit your laborers. Witness the strikes and labor troubles that beset your factories!"

And the answer of the industrialist comes quick and cutting, "Our laborers were formerly tenants on your farms, working physically apart from each other, with no bargaining power, helpless to enforce the laws designed to give them their just share, jobless six months between planting and harvest. We took them into our factories on year-round employment, put them to work under one roof so they can discuss their common problems and unite to bargain collectively and effectively. Yes, we fought them in the light of self-interest over the bargaining table, but at least they can fight back on equal terms — which is more than they can do as feudal serfs. Whatever is the outcome, they will get more wages than they did as tenants — still we are glad for they have more to spend on the goods we manufacture. The number of jobs we offer will multiply as their families grow — not like the land that is forever the same in the area and yield."

The feudalist waxes professorial. "Haven't you heard of the classical school for economic thought? Of laissez-faire, free trade, and survival of the fittest?"

131

And the industrialist answers with patient forebearance. "My dear fellow, such ideas have been embalmed and buried along with Adam Smith and 19th century England. England did pursue a policy of government noninterference, because she was mistress of the seas and trade routes and had an industrial economy second to none. She preached the gospel of free trade and survival of the fittest because she was an industrial collossus among backward nations. She is no longer. It is now America's turn to preach free trade."

The industrialist continues, "Asking an underdeveloped country like the Philippines to stake its economy in the arena of world trade is like asking a baby to make his own living in competition among adults, like forcing a flyweight boxer to fight in the heavyweight division. Oh no, let us retire to our training camp and develop ourselves first. Let us develop our industries, make finished goods out of our own natural resources and for our own consumption. Then let us export our surplus goods (but not raw materials) in competition with other industrialized nations on an equal and reciprocal basis."

Perhaps, in the industrialist, lies our hope for the future.

THE SOCIO-ECONOMIC PROGRAM

Look at it and note it well — 130 pages of dirty brown paper, bound with a Bates fastener, mimeographed in cheap ink, in letters almost illegible. Read through it if you care to, if you can grasp the ponderosity of ideas too vast and complex, of words too abstract and vague, of numerical figures that resemble mileages between the stars and stretch far beyond your imagination.

For most of you who care and dare, the reading of this document they call the "Five-Year Integrated Socio-Economic Development Program," forbiding as it may first appear, will challenge your imagination and your peace of mind. It will usher into view the shape of things to come, beyond the problem of next day's menu, homework, or employment interview. It will paint for you magnificent castles in the air, under which the necessary foundations await the stroke of willing hands.

As a program, it means nothing more than eight different economic programs meant in the past. It is nothing more than the setting up of target goals, target dates, and the government policies that are meant to bring them about. It is nothing more than what other presidents did before President Macapagal — except for one thing:

Other presidents did not live long enough or procrastinated too much. Their programs were never fully crystallized until the power to act almost effectively passed out of their hands. President Macapagal is probably the first president of the Philippines who had a specific economic program at the outset of his administration, and who acted decisively on it on the first day he assumed office. In doing so, he served notice that economic progress shall henceforth be the supreme and overriding objective of his administration.

What is the role of private enterprise in the Socio-Economic Program?

"The task of economic development belongs principally to private enterprise and not to the government . . . the role of the government is to create a favorable environment for and to assist private business in the performance of its rightful task of developing the country and its resources . . ."

Filipino businessmen and industrialists have in many ways taken up the challenge of the administration to contribute to the great task of nation building.

Already whole complexes of steel and base metals, basic chemicals, paper making, and basic food processing are beginning to dominate the skyline of 1965.

Already, spectacular advances are being registered in finance and marketing. The insatiable demand for capital and markets have spurred the formation of investment houses, rural and development banks, management companies, mergers and combinations, nationwide chain stores, and wholesale outlets.

Already, prophets in business suits conspire against traditions irrelevant to the modern day world, turning lavish fiestas into vehicles for capital formation.

To us, this is the time of high adventure, a history-laden time comparable to that of England after the repeal of the Corn Laws and to that of the United States at the close of the Civil War. It is the time of the Rockefellers, the Vanderbilts, the Morgans, and the Fords. It is truly the time of our Industrial Revolution.

But the extent to which the private businessmen and the industrialist will succeed in bringing to fruition the socio-economic program, will depend on what happens in this session of Congress.

For betwixt the cup and the lip is many a slip; and with the advent of decontrol, many a slip is scandalously showing —

Tax-free import privileges for foreign goods by a host of government agencies and private institutions; undervaluation and smuggling of foreign goods under the aegis of a law that shows no teeth; legalized usury worthy of Shylock; open-door policies toward colonial traders and foreign monopolists in combination and conspiracy to restrain free competition; and strait jacket laws of every conceivable contrivance dedicated to the proposition that industrialization is a conspiracy against the consumer.

If Congress does not act soon enough, with the ever increasing flow of foreign products subsidized at the expense of job opportunities for our people — the years to come will be for the Filipino, not the Years of Plenty but the Years of the Wistful Window Shopping.

But all will not be lost. We, the Filipino people, count very little in the scheme of things, as individuals. But collectively, we have mighty power. We have the power of purchase to make or break business empires. We have the power of the vote to raise or topple governments. We have the power to shape the future, our own future — if we can see that far ahead and if we know the road that leads to it.

The Integrated Socio-Economic Development Program does show us the way, if we are willing to follow it, if we are willing to conspire with God Himself to shape our economic destiny.

What did Omar Khayyam say?

If you and I with Him conspire
To grasp this sorry scheme of things entire,
Would we not shatter it to bits —
And then remold it to our heart's desire.

——— o———

WITHOUT FEAR OF TOMORROW
(*with apologies to Norman Corwin*)

You, young college graduate, whose path to learning is paved by the sweat of your brow and your father's lifetime savings, — in whose hands, as it were, lay the hopes of your forebears long bound to feudal servitude — you become part of the growing army of the jobless, bitter and disillusioned, and you see no future farther than the next employment interview.

You, businessman, holding your head above a sea of mounting debts, seeking government help that is given and taken away in an endless nerve-wracking game of life and death — you say: "What is the use of investing in land, buildings and machinery that give my money back in 20 years when I see no future farther than my next appointment at the local bank?"

You, housewife, voiceless victim of bill-collectors, money-lenders and profiteers, locked in the daily struggle with hunger and high prices — you find every tomorrow creep in this petty pace till the end of the month when comes the paycheck which never, never seems enough.

You, Filipino, child of the land of the morning, ever within whose skies you seek the radiance of economic liberty — what do you see in your future save uncertainty and fear?

Well, take your mind's eye out of low range, whisk it high up above the gathering clouds of conflict, and witness a silent, unremitting war that is being fought here in the Philippines, as it has been fought many times before in many other countries — in England during the repeal of the Corn Laws, in America during and after the Civil War, in Japan under Emperor Meiji, in Turkey under Kemal Ataturk, in Germany under Bismarck. It is an industrial revolution against the forces of feudal stagnation.

136

On one side are the forces of the past — the caciques and the colons — the landed aristocracy and the foreign colonial traders, whose interest lies in the perpetuation of a plantation type of import-export economy. On the other, a new middle class of factory owners, industrial workers and professionals who carry their revolution against the past on two mighty movements: Nationalism and Industrialization.

The Filipino people will have a hard time choosing sides. The vague, vast and complex economic theories, spelled out in abstract and technical language will defy understanding. There will be confusion among ranks of the combatants, among caciques who are also industrialists and industrialists who are also importers. But more and more, the lines of battle will be drawn clear.

And you, the voter and consumer, will choose the victor through the goods you purchase and the candidates you vote for.

Tomorrow — who knows?

But tonight, when you come home from your place of work, dear reader, and lay your head on your pillow to claim the rest you earned at the eighth of a long day — between the closing of your eyes and the coming of sleep, in that twilight zone of wakefulness where thoughts and plans and prayers dwell —

Think. Think of the role you play in the great task before us — ushering our nation out of benighted centuries of feudal stagnation into the light of day of 20th century progress and enlightment.

Plan. Measure out new opportunities, that none shall suffer for lack of work, and that hope shall come sooner than posterity has a right to expect.

And pray . . . .

Lord God of income tax and minimum wage,
  Who has feathered the cock against the time of
    typhoon —
  Do bring sweet influences to bear upon the produc-
    tion line;
  Accept the smoke of the factories among the ac-
    credited clouds of the sky;
  Lead us not into the arena of world trade
  As hewers of wood and suppliers of raw material;
  But give us the time and patience to develop our
    industrial skills
  That our nation may survive with dignity among
    the fittest.
Lord God of Mount Sinai and investigating committees,
  Whose terrible wrath smote the money changers at
    the temple —
  Unsheathe once more Thy avenging sword
  Against grafters and political apportunists,
  Unscrupulous landlords, capitalists, carpet-baggers,
  Dishonest labor leaders and all the economic
    parasites
  Who fatten their bellies on the fruits of another
    man's labor.
Lord God of feast and famine,
  Who changed water into wine at Cana —
  Reverse now thy miracle in our festive towns and
    barrios;
  Change the tuba and the coca-cola
  Into tears and honest sweat;
  Above all —
  Give him whom You have made in Your image
  The strength of mind and will to work,
  The strength of heart and hand
  To wield the hammer and the plow,
  That he may live today
  Without fear of tomorrow . . . .

Amen.

———o———

THE PHILOSOPHY OF
ECONOMIC NATIONALISM*

It is with a deep sense of humility that I accept the degree of doctor of economics, *honoris causa*, from this eminent institution. I am quite conscious, to paraphrase Sir Winston Churchill somewhat loosely, that I do not in the least deserve this honor; rather, it was thrust upon me. And if this doctoral hood weighs somewhat heavily on my shoulders, it is because it carries the tremendous weight of a university that stands as an eloquent symbol of our nation's future. It also carries the weight of a man who for the past decade and a half has influenced the course of economic thought and policies in this country, and who, over and above his diverse business interests, places top priority on the growth and development of the University he founded. I refer to its President, Dr. Salvador Araneta.

If I may be permitted to digress briefly, I do remember with a certain degree of fondness that Dr. Araneta gave me my very first job after I was graduated from college. He hired me to head the Feati University graduate school of Management Engineering.

I was not the only one so favored. There were many of us so favored by Dr. Araneta, specially in the early 1950's when Araneta was a cabinet member many times over and already a legendary national figure. He used to gather together young brilliant minds, talk to them, teach them and indoctrinate them with his ideas and ideals. Among these young men were Leonides Virata, now a

---

* Speech delivered by Hon. Hilarion M. Henares, Jr., Chairman, National Economic Council, at the Commencement Exercises and Solemn Investiture of the Araneta University wherein he was conferred the degree of Doctor of Economics, Honoris Causa, on May 15, 1965, at the Philamlife Auditorium.

139

financier and entrepreneur; Jose B. Fernandez, president of the Far East Bank; Sixto Roxas, consultant and former NEC Chairman; Antonio de Joya, the advertising executive; Washington Sycip, the head of the largest accounting firm in the whole Far East; and even Armand Fabella, the head of the Program Implementation Agency.

I remember how he used to gather us young men just out of college and draft us into committees to study the various ideas he advanced in the higher councils of state. I do remember with fondness when one day all of us, more in mischief than in malice, decided to outvote Dr. Araneta, our chairman, saying "We are sorry, Dr. Araneta, but we cannot agree with your views. Since we outvote you, perhaps you will give us the liberty of drafting the committee report which we are hereby submitting to you" — to test the mettle of leadership of this great man.

Dr. Araneta read our report quietly and ominously. Then he stood up, his figure looming twice as large as any single one of us and with a voice cracking like the thunder of the Lord, said:

"Boys, you did a very good job. I will tell you what I am going to do. I am going to attach your report as an appendix to *my* report!"

Of course, Dr. Araneta was exaggerating. When the day of reckoning came, our report found its way into Dr. Araneta's *footnotes* — which illustrates the lesson of a Chinese proverb which says: "The world will stand aside for any man who knows where he is going."

I am quite elated by the fact that I have been honored by no less than an educational institution that has never been embarrassed, and in fact has been fiercely proud of its nationalistic orientation. For Araneta University is truly a Filipino University; its values and its outlook represent not only the highest but also the most urgent Filipino ideals. Its very character is that it is a training ground for men, from technicians to leaders, who will

140

eventually give their full share to the agricultural and industrial development of the country.

From these remarks, you will perhaps appreciate why I feel a special sense of pride in the link that has just been forged between this institution and myself. All during the past years, when Dr. Araneta, in conjunction with the great voice of the late Senator Claro M. Recto, was espousing the cause of nationalism in what seemed to be an isolated chorus, I was one of those who devoured their ideas with the voracity of a young student learning from more mellowed minds. I am not quite sure that older leaders like Dr. Araneta now consider me an adequate exponent of economic nationalism, but they will have to admit that I am the most talkative!

Considering the character of this University, this is perhaps the best occasion for restating in brief the premises, the substance, the content of economic nationalism, a movement which only a few years ago was considered a dangerous force that had better be suppressed, but has now emerged as the prime moving spirit of this country. I have a feeling that those who belittle, oppose or malign this movement have not made the slightest effort to appreciate it in its true light. With your leave, I shall attempt to expose the soul of this force in as straightforward a manner as possible and in as simple a language as possible.

For I do remember the words of one of my Jesuit professors, Father Mulry, who once said to me:

"Mr. Henares, in promulgating your esoteric cogitations or articulating your sentimentalities, beware of platitudinous ponderosity. Eschew all conglomerations of flatulent garrulity, jejune babblement and asinine affectation. Avoid all polysyllabic profundity, setacious vacuity and grandiloquent vapidity.

"In other words, Mr. Henares, speak frankly, simply, plainly and above all, *avoid using big words!*"

For big words, Father Mulry said, does not necessarily reflect grand thoughts. And it should be the pre-

141

sumptuous ambition of all of us to be said of us as once was said of Winston Churchill:

"By saying simply and plainly what we feel, he has enabled us to feel it still more strongly; and by the power of his words, he has driven us to the limits of our potentialities, and has given us a vision of our own best possibilities."

Contrary to the claims of nonsympathizers, the objective of economic nationalism is not to restrict the foreigner in this country, but to free the Filipino in his own home. Its aim is not to constrain but to liberate. It is born not of hatred but of impatience, the impatience of a country that is young enough to be full of energies but is old enough to be able to stand alone and plot its own direction. This, without frills or distortions, is to me the very nature of economic nationalism. It stands for freedom—and freedom implies strength, not dependence. The wave of economic nationalism on whose crest we ride today is a perfectly logical part of the sweep of our history. Close to seven decades ago, nationalism was the force that bound and stirred our people into fighting for political freedom, the freedom from colonialist masters. Today it is the same force that impels us to strive for the achievement of our own economic strength.

I refer, of course, to both our internal and external strength. Our aim is the kind of strength that leaves as little area of vulnerability as possible. This is the overriding aim of government policy today, as dictated and inspired by the socio-economic development program of the President.

What do we mean by internal strength? By it we mean simply the capacity of the country to provide the needs of every single family, not only to subsist but to live a life of reasonable comfort and dignity. We are fighting a tyranny that is far more ruthless than the overt political dictatorships that abound in many parts of Asia, Europe, Africa and Latin America. We are grappling with a far more basic constraint to human freedom: the tyranny of poverty, of underdevelopment. As we look far beyond the dynamic and affluent sectors of our economy, far beyond those sectors that have commanded attention for the past decade and a half for their magnificent success in laying down the beginning of the country's industrial base, if we look far beyond them and survey the millions of households who still compose the bulk of our population, the manifestations of this tyranny cannot help but impose themselves on our sight. Their choice, their alternative, are limited; and so, by necessity, is their freedom.

A tenant farmer who lives on a simple and frugal diet of rice, vegetables, and fish, who cannot afford the expenses of giving his children the benefits of an adequate education, whose life is limited to the elemental functions of eating, working and sleeping, whose only sources of credit are either his own landlord or countryside usurers, is certainly far less free than a family man earning a high income, who lives in a comfortable house, has ample opportunities for self-improvement and for the education of his children, and is sufficiently trained to enable him to choose among alternative methods of earning a livelihood.

Our prime objective is to release our population from the bonds that restrict the majority of them and to enhance the liberty of those who already enjoy it. This can be done only by increasing the productivity of the country, or, to put it another way, the incomes earned by our people: in short, by vigorous and sustained economic development. It can be attained only by massive investments both on the part of the government and the private sector. On the government's side, it means directing a large proportion of its own resources towards building the roads, the harbors, and airports, the power systems, the telecommunication facilities, the irrigation networks, and the host of other physical social assets without which the growth of private productivity will be neither technically nor financially feasible. On the private sector's side, it means the build-up of physical capital for raising the volume and diversifying the range of products both of industry and agriculture, with a view not only towards supplying more and more of our domestic requirements from domestic sources but also establishing solid footholds in potential markets for Philippine exports abroad.

The development of such internal strength is the objective that gives substance and meaning to economic nationalism. Any economic sentiment or movement that totally ignores this objective is not only meaningless and hollow but downright dangerous. Contrary to the assertions of organized foreign propaganda, our economic nationalism is neither obsessed nor devoted to excluding the foreigner from the Philippine economy. This is an empty and uninspiring preoccupation; it is nothing more than chauvinism. Our nationalism is aimed primarily at developing internal strength, and if at the same time it shows genuine concern over the dangers of external control, it is because our domestic and external capabilities are inextricably bound together in at least two ways.

The first is that our own state of underdevelopment considerably weakens our posture in the international markets. Our bargaining strength is weak both as buyers and as sellers. As long as we limit our exports to a small group of primary and unprocessed agricultural and mineral raw materials for foreign factories and as long as the bulk of our requirements for manufactured goods come from abroad, we risk the long run prospects of our terms of trade turning against us. Moreover, as long as our exports are mostly purchased by one country and as long as our imports are mostly supplied by the same country, we shall always stand to pay the price of dependence, particularly in terms of negotiating weakness when issues come to a head on such matters as parity, tariff protection, definition of areas open to foreign investors, and others. In any case, our state of economic insufficiency renders us wide open and highly vulnerable to external economic forces and policies beyond our control. We are, in other words, still suffering from a weakness common to all former colonial economies.

Secondly, the fact that our industrial capacity is far below the level required for serving our growing population, the fact that there are critical obstacles to the mobi-

144

lization of domestic capital for industrial development, the fact that development necessarily requires foreign financing to make our growth efforts consistent with the stability both of domestic prices and the balance of payments — all of these facts make our country exposed to another peril: that of too much extraneous direction over our internal economy. On the one hand, our own condition increases the temptation to relegate the task of domestic development to foreign capital and foreign entrepreneurs. On the other hand, the attractive potential offered by the Philippine economy has been and will always be an irresistible temptation to foreign capital to establish its own footholds within this country. This condition places us in an old dilemma: are we willing to pay the price of foreign economic dominance even if such dominance brings with it a higher rate of investment and growth? Are the benefits worth the cost?

The answer really depends on another question: do we have other alternatives or not? The answer is yes, we do. We need not succumb in order to grow. We need not pay the price of subjection in order to develop. We have right here in our country the entrepreneurs who can build and expand the industries of the future. We have right here in our country an impressive amount of available capital for investment into productive ventures. And although we admittedly need foreign financing to support our growth, we have right here in our country the enlightened leadership both in the government and in the private sectors to make sure that foreign capital will come to this country *on our own terms*. We have the necessary resources and facilities to develop the country intensively, to develop it rapidly, and most of all, to develop it according to our own aspirations. We certainly have the means; all we need is the will.

We have in our midst a veritable powerhouse of business leaders — the Aranetas, the Sorianos, the Ayalas, the Elizaldes, the Palancas, the Tuasons, the Ysmaels, the Del Rosarios, the Puyats and all the entrepreneurs, big and small, who have laid the country's productive base during the last decade and a half. I am not convinced that we should ignore the moving power of these men and call on total strangers to do our development work for us. I am not convinced that foreign nationals are better attuned to the highest aspirations of our people than our own businessmen are. I am not convinced that foreign capital can interpret the best interests of the Filipino better than we can. Nor am I convinced that they shall put our own national interest over and above their own. The firmest tenet of economic nationalism is that the Filipino should be the primary agent and beneficiary of his country's economic progress. And the firmest hope of economic nationalism is that the Filipino has the capacity, the talent, and the aggressiveness for it.

There is another problem to be settled: can the country muster enough capital from within to finance its large investment requirements? I do not think anyone will dispute that the potential is there.

Within the past three years, there has been a shift in the flow of income largely due to the adjustment in the exchange rate. While corporate profits in the manufacturing sectors have been going through a squeeze due to upward adjustments in costs, the incomes in the agricultural and export sectors have swelled due to the higher conversion rates of export earnings. While perhaps the present industrial sector is not as promising a source of savings as it used to be, the areas enjoying the benefits of decontrol have considerably increased their saving potential.

This is made even more true by the fact that these increases in incomes are largely concentrated on a well identifiable sector of our economy. This group, in fact, has so much liquidity that their problem is to seek attractive investment outlets and, finding none, throw their funds instead into real estate, unnecessary consumption expenses, travel, and other forms of unproductive expenditures. If there were indeed a shortage of capital, I fail to see how construction can go through such a vigorous boom as it had enjoyed during the past years, and I fail to see how land values can rise so fast in various commer-

146

cial, residential, and even vacation resort areas throughout the country. If there were a dryness of capital, I fail to see how so much foreign exchange can flow out of the country under all sorts of indivisible categories.

No, I do not believe that our problem is the lack of investible resources. This is certainly an invalid ground for forfeiting our economy entirely to foreign capital. The investible funds are available from local sources: the problem is to induce them to flow into new, basic, and integrated ventures.

Here, we go into the role of the legislature in assisting the cause of economic nationalism. Congressional assistance is certainly an indispensable instrument in giving muscle to this movement. For the only way to build an economy of Filipinos, by Filipinos and for Filipinos is to give compelling incentives to Filipino capital to assume the essential function of risk-taking and path-breaking. These it will not do unless existing laws are changed, present bottlenecks removed and positive inducements provided. We cannot emphasize the necessity for a clear-cut investments incentives law, spelling out the areas that would be given top priority and specifying without ambiguity the types of concessions and benefits which risktakers in these areas will enjoy. Our existing tax and tariff laws, for example, are obsolete from the point of view of current requirements. Our tax laws hardly give any special treatment to risktakers and our tariff laws no longer reflect the pattern of protection we want to establish for our existing and new industries.

Such an investments incentives law should not stop, however, at simply giving inducements to Filipinos to venture into new enterprises. It should also lay down the terms and conditions under which foreign financial resources are to participate in our economic development. No one, I think, would be so naive as to deny our need for foreign capital to finance part of our economic development. Neither our domestic savings rate, our international reserves, our balance of payments, nor our exchange rate will be able to sustain our development efforts purely

147

from domestic financing. But we cannot afford to leave the country completely open to external forces. Our task is to make sure that we use foreign resources to the maximum advantage without necessarily surrendering our sovereignty and supremacy over our own economy.

And this is where the economic nationalist gets to be sensitively jealous of the Filipinos' rights and prerogatives in his own country. It is not in accord with our long-run interests to have critical areas in industry dominated by wholly owned subsidiaries of foreign-based parent companies, in which Filipinos have no share in the ownership nor in critical management decisions. It is not in accord with our long-run interest to have foreign-owned financial institutions enjoying advantages over their Filipino-owned counterparts. It is not in accord with our long-run interests to have absolutely no power to choose which prerogatives shall be reserved exclusively for Filipinos without being legally obliged to extend the same to the nationals of another country by virtue of an agreement imposed on us during a moment of weakness and dire need.

I do not think that anybody can rightfully brand our kind of nationalism as extremist. In the last analysis, it is nothing more than an overdue assertion of Filipino dignity. There is nothing unreasonable in seeking to change our external economic relationships in a manner that restores to the Filipino the undisputed supremacy he has by right over his own land, where he is bound to live all his life. This is a right that is strictly respected and protected by the governments and citizens of such countries as the United States, Great Britain, France, Canada, Germany, Japan and other sovereign countries all throughout the world. The Filipino wishes to do no less.

What, in summary, does the economic nationalist stand for?

First, he stands for a rapid rate of economic development: for a vigorous expansion of the country's productive capacity, for a sustained increase in the people's

148

incomes, and for the spread of the fruits of growth among the mass of our population. The nationalist, in other words, stands for upliftment.

Second, he stands for the perfectly logical principle that the Philippine economy belongs to Filipinos and should move in the direction that Filipinos want. This implies that Filipinos should be in predominant control of the productive assets, of the distribution networks, and of the financial institutions in his own country.

Third, he stands for partnership with foreign capital in the development of the Philippine economy, a partnership based on mutual respect and dignity and on the recognition of Filipino supremacy over his own land. We are and shall always be hospitable to foreign capital, just as we are and shall always be hostile to foreign control.

This is the substance of the nationalist's faith. It is my only hope that this faith—with the help of such institutions as the Araneta University and under the inspiring leadership of its President—shall grow as the moving force of this country in the ensuing decades and lead our people to the fulfillment of their highest aspirations.

We are more than economic nationalists, we must remember that above all, we are Filipinos.

As Filipinos, we should love our country above any other, no matter how friendly, wealthy or powerful. We must protect and defend and promote the interest of our country and our citizens just as assiduously as foreign embassies protect and defend and promote the interest of their own country and citizens.

We must have Love — not only "Love for the Philippines" as Raul Manglapus would have it, whatever that means — but something else vastly different and infinitely more important, more Christian and more democratic — *Love for the Filipino.*

Not only love, but faith. We must have faith, *Faith in the Filipino*, faith in his capacity for greatness, faith

149

in his competence to take care of his own affairs. We must never join the game of national self-flagellation, by which we credit to another nation whatever is good about ourselves, and we admit that whatever is bad about our country is our own miserable fault.

We must never let pass unchallenged any alien-induced notion that the destiny of our country lies in the hands of those other than ourselves. For we must have confidence in ourselves if we are to earn the confidence of others. And in the great drama of nation-building, we Filipinos must assume the starring role; everyone else, including our foreign friends, must be in the supporting cast.

Not only love, not only faith, but also hope.

We must preach hope. For we who would transform a nation, we who would renovate a stagnant society, we cannot do so by driving our people to despair as most of our politicians and writers are doing — or by stirring up and captaining discontent — or by infecting our people with fear, hatred, distrust and self-doubt — or by submitting ourselves in humility and in humiliation to the guidance and judgment of foreign mentors.

No, we must — like the prophets of old — kindle and fan an *extravagant hope,* based on faith in ourselves if we are to inspire our people to constructive action.

Kennedy once said: "There are many of us who see things as they really are, and ask ourselves — why? But we must dream of things that never were, and ask ourselves — why not?

Now there is the difference between the merely curious and the boldly adventurous. The curious see things as they really are and ask "Why?" almost despairingly. The adventurous dream of things that never were and ask "why not?"

And indeed, why not? In all ages, times and climes, men fought most valiantly for things that never were, for gardens yet to be planted and cities yet to be built, for beautiful women yet to be loved, for heavenly kingdoms yet to be won, and for new nations yet to be born! Dreams, visions, and wild hopes are mighty weapons in the hands of those who plunge into undertakings of great change.

Not only love, faith and hope — but also involvement. We must agitate the very core of the national spirit. We must usher our people into a sense of self-involvement, a sense of conscious participation in the actions and passions of our times, remembering the words of one philosopher who said:

"There are no great men. There are only great challenges which fate forces ordinary men to face."

My young friends, for those of you who are about to graduate, a special message.

When you go out of the door of this University into the wide open world, your life's journey has just begun. And if you keep forever young, just like Dr. Araneta here and, if I may add, like my father out there, somewhere in the audience — if you keep forever young as they do, then the thrill, the wonder and the excitement of your life's journey will never end.

To paraphrase General McArthur, "Youth is not entirely a time of life. It is a state of mind. It is not wholly a matter of ripe cheeks, red lips and supple knees. It is a temper of the will, a quality of the imagination, a vigor of the emotions, a freshness in the springs of life."

And my young friends, "Nobody grows old by merely living a number of years. People grow old only by deserting their ideals. The years may wrinkle the skin but to give up interest in life wrinkles the soul. Worry, doubt, distrust, fear, despair — these are the long years that bow the head and turn the growing spirit to dust."

My young friends, you are only as young as your faith and as old as your doubts. You are only as young as your self confidence and as old as your fears. You are only as young as your hopes, and as old as your despair.

151

"In a central place in your heart, there is a recording chamber. For as long as it receives messages of beauty, of hope, of cheer and courage — for as long as it does that — then you are young.

"When the wires are all down and the heart is covered with the snow of pessimism and the ice of cynicism — when your hearts begin to fill with fear, hatred, distrust and self-doubt — then, and only then, my young friends, are you grown old."

With this hope I depart: May you be forever young as your President Salvador Araneta is and will always be.

May his ideas and ideals live within you and through you unto your issue — there to multiply a thousand, a million times fold, till they sweep across the land and shape the destiny of our nation.

I have no doubt that this will happen. I know, because I, too, have been under the influence of this great man. And someday soon, not yet perhaps, but sooner than we expect, according to his vision, God will walk upon this earth on brown legs.

As one Filipino poet once expressed it:

> *Not yet, Rizal, not yet;*
> *Sleep not in peace.*
> *There are a thousand waters to be spanned;*
> *There are a thousand bridges to be crossed;*
> *There are a thousand crosses to be borne.*
>
> *Not yet, not yet;*
> *The glory hour will come;*
> *Out of the silent dreaming, from the seven*
> *thousand fold silence,*
> *We shall emerge, saying: We are Filipinos—*
> *And no longer be ashamed.*

THE MONETARY AND FISCAL SITUATION*
(1965)

Introduction: The End of Controls

The character of the monetary and fiscal situation in the Philippines today is determined by certain basic changes that have taken place in the economy during the past two-and-a-half years. The Philippines in 1965 was still experiencing both the benefits and the agonies of devaluation. After a long period of exchange controls (imposed in 1949), which maintained the official exchange rate at ₱2.00 to $1.00 (U.S.) through a tight system of exchange rationing, a program of "gradual decontrol" was initiated in 1960 and culminated in 1962.

Domestic inflationary expenditures during the second half of the 1950's, traceable in a large part to an aggressive fiscal sector and the resultant growth of bank liquidity, had driven the official rate out of line with the equilibrium rate. This "overvaluation" of the peso in terms of foreign currencies, in its turn, led to an aggravation of the balance of payments disequilibrium and the expansion of the black market in foreign exchange. It also led to the emergence of overcapacities in later-stage (processing and finishing) manufacturing industries, where the bulk of assets utilized were imported semi-processed materials and where profitability depended to a large extent on the effective exchange subsidy granted to authorized importations.

The gradual decontrol program launched in 1960 — and originally planned as a four-year adjustment process — initially established a multiple rate system which sought to adjust the exchange rates nearer equilibrium, and which provided a system of preferred rates to preferred imports. In January 1962, two years ahead of schedule, the newly-elected administration abruptly abolished the entire sys-

* Prepared for the Third Rehovoth Conference, Israel, August, 1965.

tem of exchange controls. The measure taken was, in effect, twofold. First, the administrative licensing of virtually every foreign exchange transaction was lifted, and a free market was established. Second, the exchange rate was allowed to seek its own level under a system where the rate was permitted to fluctuate freely. The rate was thereby effectively (but not formally) devalued from the official ₱2.00 : $1.00 to the current ₱3.90 : $1.00. This "free" rate has been relatively stable since mid-1962 due largely to extensive Central Bank support of the market.

The one exception to the lifting of controls was the requirement that 20% of gross export proceeds should be surrendered to the Central Bank at the official par value, which remains at ₱2.00 : $1.00. The rest may be freely negotiated and converted at the going rate.

Simultaneous with decontrol, the government launched a Five-Year Integrated Programme for Social and Economic Development.

Effects of Decontrol

1. The immediate effect of decontrol was a marked improvement in the balance of trade. After more than a decade of chronic trade deficits, the negative gap narrowed in 1962 and then turned into a surplus in 1963. However, although the fundamental payments disequilibrium resulting from an unrealistic rate was removed, the pressures on international reserve persisted, but for entirely different reasons (see No. 6, below). These pressures are a major factor behind the tenor of official monetary policies in the Philippines.

2. As anticipated, decontrol induced a massive shift in cost structures and income flows. The agricultural and mineral sectors serving the export market enjoyed a basic upward adjustment in peso incomes due to the higher conversion rate. The 20% retention mentioned above was imposed partly to cushion the inflationary pressure coming from this source. At the current exchange rate, the 20% retention is an effective 10% "tax" on gross export revenues.[1]

3. The profitability of certain import-based manufacturing sectors, on the other hand, took a downward adjustment, with some vulnerable sectors verging towards a crisis. The severity of the income squeeze depended on the extent to which their materials were imported.[2]

4. Their problems were not confined to their earnings but to their balance sheets as well. The debt on equipment imported at the old exchange rate under long-term deferred payment arrangements had now to be amortized at the higher exchange rate. The increased cost of importation plus the upward revaluation of foreign exchange liabilities generated a need for new funds.

5. The legislature provided some relief to industry by a number of tax-exemption measures. It has not, however, acted favorably on legislation to shift some of the tax burden onto the areas benefited by the decontrol.

6. Exchange controls had been used during the 1950's as an instrument of commercial policy as well as protection through the expedient of directing dollar allocations towards the establishment and operation of preferred industries and limiting allocations to finished-goods importations. The removal of controls, therefore, shifted the onus of protection towards tariff policy, the enforcement of which has met with administrative difficulties. Clandestine and disguised importations that circumvent tariffs not only

---

[1] Of every $5.00 of export receipts, $4.00 (or 80%) are converted at the rate of ₱3.90, and the proceeds amount to ₱15.60, while $1.00 (or 20%) is converted at the rate of ₱2.00. The total proceeds, therefore, run up to ₱17.60, and average proceeds per dollar are about ₱3.50. The difference between this and the current rate, amounting to ₱0.40, represents an equivalent disinflationary levy of 10% (on ₱3.90). It is not, however, a tax in the full sense, for it is not channeled as revenue to the government. It is a Central Bank levy and becomes, in effect, a sterilized surplus, although it is booked under the "revaluation of international reserve" account.

---

[2] There are notable exceptions. The construction industry and those serving it have been thriving due to continued availability of credit from large but conservative insurance institutions (public and private) and to the persevering strength of investor preference for ventures based on real estate and commercial buildings. The appliance industries are penetrating the middle-class market with the assistance of sales finance companies.

use up the country's foreign exchange reserves but also flood the domestic market with finished goods that undersell local products.

Monetary and Fiscal Policy

Given these circumstances, monetary policy has been largely defensive against unduly feeding the increased demand for credit and inducing raids on the foreign exchange reserve. It has, in general, imposed tight restraints on commercial bank credit expansion. The fiscal sector, on the other hand, has suffered from short-falls in revenues and financed its deficits largely from monetized debt, i.e., credits from the Central Bank and the commercial banking system.

The orientation of monetary policy, it may be said, is predominantly dictated by three factors.

The first is the need for managing the level and the movements of the international reserve and the stabilization of the exchange rate. With the abolition of direct exchange controls, the instruments for international reserve management have shifted to the less direct and more general kind, namely, the tempered regulation of domestic expenditures by means of internal credit restraint.

In an economy like the Philippines, the propensity to import is high — both by virtue of consumer preference and by virtue of productive structures. A substantial proportion, for instance, of funds (earned or borrowed) for raw materials and good-in-process inventories are expended on imports — a major source of industrial inputs. The international reserve, for this reason, is rather sensitive to internal credit liberalization or restriction.

The second is the need for keeping domestic price levels stable, particularly the prices of foodstuffs. This objective requires both the containment of the volume of money and credit, together, however, with the extension of official financing to government consumer subsidy programs for rice and other food items. These have to be

156

imported in substantial amounts by the Rice and Corn Agency (RCA) and by the National Marketing Corporation (NAMARCO) to help meet consumption requirements. A substantial subsidy likewise goes to the production of tobacco.

The third is the increasing difficulty of the government to meet its disbursement requirements (both operating and developmental) from tax revenue collections, thus pressing the Central Bank to extend credit and overdraft facilities to finance government budgetary deficits.

One cause for the insufficiency of tax revenues has just been mentioned: the passage by Congress of a number of tax-exemption measures without the legislation of new taxes to offset the loss in collections. Another reason is the cessation of the margin fee on foreign exchange purchases. A further cause, and an important one, is the failure to redistribute the tax burden in the light of income shifts after decontrol. There are administrative difficulties in collecting taxes out of agricultural incomes, for this sector's operations are not as well-documented as those of the industrial and mining sectors. On the whole, the legislature has resisted the attempts of the administration to have new tax measures passed, including bills imposing an export tax (to catch part of the increase in post-decontrol peso earnings), increasing corporate income tax rates, and increasing taxes on gasoline and diesel.

The revenue-expenditure gap has to be met by borrowings. The securities market in the Philippines, however, is relatively limited and has not provided extensive facilities for public issues of government debt instruments to tap non-bank sources of funds. Moreover, the overwhelming proportion of government bonds issued for development purposes pay rates (4%) that are unrealistic in terms of the going cost of money in the country, and thus meet with little public response except from commercial banks. The incentives of the latter to hold these bonds are threefold: (a) the bonds are eligible as bank reserves to meet legal reserve requirements, subject to certain limitations;[3] (b) the price of bonds are supported at par by the Central Bank, eliminating the danger of capital loss; and (c) the bonds are readily saleable to the Central Bank, thus allowing banks to earn on reserve and excess funds without sacrificing liquidity and the integrity of the investment.

In the absence of other purchasers, the Central Bank thus becomes the largest single holder of government securities (about 44%) and the whole banking system (the CB and commercial banks) hold about 67% of total government issues.[4] Most of the rest are absorbed by government trust funds and government non-bank financial institutions. The private sector holds about 2%.

Deficits, therefore, tend to be monetized, both by bank absorptions of bond issues as well as by direct Central Bank advances and overdraft facilities extended to the government. These requirements compel the Central Bank to adopt a posture of restraint towards commercial bank credit to keep over-all liquidity within the bounds of stability.

Measures of Monetary Restraint

In the absence of an export tax, the Central Bank has continued to maintain the 20% retention on export proceeds, mentioned above, as a substitute disinflationary measure as well as a source of foreign exchange for market support purposes.

A succession of restraining measures on commercial bank credit were promulgated starting in 1962 by the Central Bank. These were in the nature of traditional in-

---

[3] Bank reserves in the Philippines may be held in a prescribed combination of the following assets: cash-in-vault, deposit at the Central Bank, eligible Philippine government securities, and eligible foreign balances and U.S. securities.

[4] In 1963, an initial attempt was made to develop a public market for government securities by a ₱50 million issue of non-supported 7% ten-year bonds, with only a qualified success. Early in 1965, the government tested its credit in Foreign markets by a $15 million issue of 6½ fifteen-year bonds for water facilities projects. The issue was highly successful.

struments: increases in legal reserve requirements,[5] raising of the rediscount rate (from 3% to 6% in 1962), and the reimposition of rediscount quotas for commercial banks based on their net worth. Commercial bank credit, however, expanded by 13.3% in 1962 and by 24.7% in 1963; aggregate credits of the banking system (including the Central Bank) increased by 11.4% in 1962 and 22.8% in 1963; and money supply rose by 12.9% in 1962 and by an unprecedented 18.0% in 1963. The consumer price index in Manila went up by 8.7% in 1962 and 7.9% in 1963.

In view of these expansionary developments, the Central Bank — in conjunction with the fiscal authorities — took a series of tightening measures in 1964 on the banking system, the severity of which has had no precedent. The heaviest measure was the removal of some ₱100 million of government time and savings deposits from private commercial banks. Early in 1965, government current operating accounts with private banks were also closed. These represented a massive withdrawal of reserves from these depository banks. The Central Bank provided some compensatory measures by making emergency advances to the commercial banks amounting to half of the savings and time deposits withdrawn. These advances matured early in 1965.

The remaining government deposits were subjected to additional constraints. A ceiling was imposed on government deposits which an individual bank may hold. A "liquidity floor" provision was promulgated, requiring banks to hold government bonds equal to 30% of government deposits, over and above the ordinary reserve requirements. This liquidity floor was raised to 100% in June 1965. This liquidity floor, of course, was tantamount to an effective increase in reserve requirement. Rediscount quotas, however, were increased in May 1964 and again in May 1965.

---

[5] In 1962, the legal reserve requirement against demand deposits was raised from 15% to 19%. In 1963, the reserve requirement against savings and time deposits was increased from 5% to 6%. In 1965, the requirement was unified to 10% for all deposits. All the while, a 100% requirement has been in force on special time deposits required for opening letters of credit.

The severity of the measures are reflected in the drastic drop of ₱350.5 million (a 12% decrease) in the money supply from the end of December 1963 to July 1964, a seven-month period. As of April 1965, it has not yet recovered its previous level.

All these measures came at a time of heavy demand for funds, for reasons already cited at the beginning. The banking system could not quite liquidate its portfolio — in spite of the large reserve drains — for two reasons. First, the companies that had outstanding loans were, to a large extent, also suffering from a liquidity shortage, as already mentioned. Second, the banking system, historically, had supported the growth of manufacturing industries during the period of controls by filling in the role of long-term creditors in the absence of institutions for providing industrial long-term finance. It was a role that could not be reversed abruptly without painful repercussions, precisely at a time when the need for funds had grown.

The readjustment, therefore, took the form not of loan-liquidation but of the infusion into the banking system of funds borrowed from the Central Bank. Loans and advances from the Central Bank now constitute a far larger proportion of bank funds than are normal in, say, the United States. Outstanding bank loans today are larger than deposits, and are thus partly financed from non-deposit funds. Transactions on the inter-bank call money market are heavy. The shortage of funds in comparison to demand is best seen in the various money rates prevailing in the market: 8-3/4% on bankers acceptances, 14% on prime finance company paper, and 36% on consumer credit from finance companies.

Conclusions

These recent developments indicate the cautious and uncompromising conservatism of monetary policy in the Philippines, a conservatism that is — on the whole — responsible for the relative stability of the country during most of its experience with central banking (although at the expense, some say, of what could have been a faster growth rate). But Philippine experience in monetary management, particularly during the period of post-decontrol readjustments, has dramatized the limitations of monetary policy (in the sense of strictly Central Bank action), more so in the absence of a widespread and sophisticated financial market. *It cannot, of itself, cope with problems of structural change.*

In the aggregate, for example, the flexibility of monetary management is conditioned by the strength of the fiscal sector. Where, for any reason, the government cannot finance its operations from non-inflationary sources of funds, the monetary agency almost always has to give priority to meeting fiscal requirements, and at the same time enforcing restraints elsewhere. Without the help of fiscal instruments (principally taxation) for regulating the flow and structure of income and savings, monetary policy can, at best, assume the passive role of imposing restrictions where it *can* do so in order to prevent any undue rise in prices or pressures on the balance of payments. Such a residual recourse may place the restraints on sectors that are not in the best position to bear them.

All this underscores the importance of taxation: its aggregate magnitudes as well as its distribution. The Philippines is quite an "undertaxed" country: tax revenues amount to only 8 to 10 per cent of national income, lower than other countries in about the same stage of development. Aggregate collections are hardly sufficient to support current operations as well as the government capital investments (principally in infrastructure) envisioned in the Five-Year Socio-Economic Programme.

Tax distribution is still relatively inequitable. The taxability of property values outside of urban areas has not quite been exploited. The well-documented industrial-mining sectors bear the brunt of income taxation while other sectors provide the traditional shelter. The 20% retention, recently sanctioned by the Supreme Court after a suit contesting its legality, is an awkward and inflexible substitute for a tax. It is, with minor exceptions, a non-

161

selective, across-the-board "levy", and the "proceeds" are sterilized by the Central Bank in a "revaluation" account. The government gets no revenues from it, although — since it is a forced saving from the economy's point of view — it gives the government that much leeway to engage in deficit spending.

The recent Philippine experience also underscores the importance of developing an effective market for government securities in order to lessen its direct dependence on the banking system for borrowed funds. But even this must presume a strong fiscal position — a strength given by an adequate tax revenue performance — since the general acceptability of government's debt instruments would depend on its financial strength. It will require the offering of a variety of securities, with differing maturities and, of course, attractive rates, to suit the needs of various investors. The existence of such a market will also enable the Central Bank to engage in open market operations (non-existent in the Philippines) on a wide and meaningful scale for purposes of influencing the volume of bank reserves as well as interest rate levels.

But the greatest discovery to be gained from the Philippine experience is the need, not just for sound monetary and fiscal policies (which, after all, are limited in scope), but for an imaginative over-all *financial* policy, reflecting the requirements both of government and of the private sector, and of existing enterprises as well as of new investments.

The changes in costs and in balance sheet (liability) values induced by the effective devaluation of the exchange rate generated a need, on the part of import-based manufacturing industries, for longer-term funds to refinance existing obligations over a longer period and to provide new working capital, as well as a need for new equity to shore up undercapitalized companies (which could live on thin equity as long as the level of profits provided by the low exchange rate were there).

The inducement of new investments and growth, likewise, will depend a complement of funds, ranging from

162

short-term debt to long-term obligations to equity, to finance the various kinds of asset structures maintained by different types of new enterprises. It need not be said that the financial structure of merchandising companies differ from that of manufacturing, and both differ from agricultural enterprises and again from public utilities. The amount and proportion of cash, receivables, inventory, and fixed assets used differ from industry to industry, and determine the various types of financing suitable for each.

Meeting their requirements, therefore, is not a simple matter of expanding bank credit (easier monetary policy) but a much more complex matter of building a variety of financial intermediaries to channel funds from sources to users in various suitable forms: short and long-term credit, secure and venture equity capital, and so on. Insurance companies abound, but their portfolios are mostly confined to policy-loans and real estate. A number of new development corporations and investment banks are now filling the gap in the financial market by placing their own funds in securities of various concerns and by underwriting issues for corporations in need for funds. These operations are still in the infant stages. A good deal of work remains to be done in organizing a widespread distribution mechanism for securities, on designing securities suitable for the market, and on gaining a wider acceptance for such financial instruments. In short, one of the most essential elements of productive growth is the development of an organized money and capital market.

This type of development would surely attract much of the funds that now merely serve to inflate real estate values, or go into commercial building construction (a booming industry), or flow out of the country. These are potential savings in search of investment outlets — outlets that can be provided only by developing the system of financial intermediaries.

THE TERMINATION OF CONSTITUTIONAL PARITY AND VESTED RIGHTS*

I. PRELIMINARY STATEMENT

For purposes of convenience two kinds of parity enjoyed by Americans under our present laws should be distinguished: *constitutional parity* as provided in the Ordinance appended to the Constitution (popularly known as the parity amendment) and reiterated, though rephrased to suit reciprocity, in Article VI, paragraph 1 of the Laurel-Langley Agreement and *business parity* as found in Article VII, paragraph 1 of the same Agreement. The former, as is well known, refers to the exploitation of the natural resources and the operation of public utilities and the latter to any form of business enterprise engaged in either by Filipinos in the United States or by Americans in the Philippines.

The concern of this Memorandum is with constitutional parity (hereafter parity), more particularly on the effects of its termination by July 3, 1974 upon rights acquired or will be acquired by Americans under its regime. Ostensibly, this will bring up the vexed question of vested rights. Preliminarily, however, the question of whether the Laurel-Langley Agreement really provides for fair and equal reciprocity will be taken up.

II. DISCUSSION

1. *Whether the provisions of the Laurel-Langley Agreement on constitutional parity satisfy the requirement of fair and equal reciprocity.*

On the merely trade aspects the Laurel-Langley Agreement seems to bestow more concessions on the Philippines

---

* Submitted to the National Economic Council in support of NEC Resolution No. 90 (65) herein appended as an appendix.

than on the United States. This, however, should not be taken as a countervailing argument for other provision or provisions in the Agreement where the United States actually enjoys the greater concession. In the first place, the fact of the Philippines having been at one time a ward of the United States entitles us to suppose that she is at least warranted in expecting greater consideration. And in the second place, even prescinding from such previous relationship, the very unequal positions of the United States and the Philippines in matters of trade and business, must naturally argue some allowance in favor of the latter.

In sharp contrast to the parity agreement of 1946 which, to say the least, was one-sided, the Laurel-Langley Agreement of 1956 established a regime of mutuality with respect to the exploitation of natural resources and the operation of public utilities. This appears in Article VI, paragraph 1, to wit:

"1. The disposition, exploitation, development, and utilization of all agricultural, timber, and mineral lands of the public domain, waters, minerals, coal, petroleum and other mineral oils, all forces and potential sources of energy, and other natural resources of either Party, and the operation of public utilities, shall, if open to any person, be open to citizens of the other Party and to all forms of business enterprise owned or controlled, directly or indirectly, by citizens of such other Party in the same manner as to and under the same conditions imposed upon citizens or corporations or associations owned or controlled by citizens of the Party granting the right.

"2. x x x

"3. The United States of America reserves the rights of the Several States of the United States to limit the extent to which citizens or corporations or associations owned or controlled by citizens of the Philippines may engage in the activities specified in this Article. The Republic of

165

the Philippines reserves the power to deny any of the rights specified in this Article to citizens of the United States who are citizens of States, or to corporations or associations at least 60 per cent of whose capital stock or capital is owned or controlled by citizens of States, which deny like rights to citizens of the Philippines, or to corporations or associations which are owned or controlled by citizens of the Philippines. The exercise of this reservation on the part of the Philippines shall not affect previously acquired rights, provided that in the event that any State of the United States of America should in the future impose restrictions which would deny to citizens or corporations or associations owned or controlled by citizens of the Philippines the right to continue to engage in activities in which they were engaged therein at the time of the imposition of such restrictions, the Republic of the Philippines shall be free to apply like limitations to the citizens or corporations or associations owned or controlled by citizens of such States.

It is on the basis of the immediately foregoing provision, however, that the disparity in the privileges of Americans and Filipinos to exploit and operate each other's natural resources and public utilities creep in. As should be obvious from the reservations, any State of the American Union enjoys complete freedom, during the life-time of the Agreement, to restrict Filipino entrepreneurship. The Philippines, on the other hand, does not enjoy any such initiative during the lifetime of the Agreement; its role, at the most, is recriminatory, so to speak. In practical terms this means that some States of the American Union, with choice possibilities of exploitation, are practically left free to shut off Filipinos anytime whereas the Philippines will remain open to American exploitation for all the time that the Agreement is in force. Doubtless, it might occur to some minds that this disparity is hardly a practical one since Filipinos are not in any financial position to exploit and operate American natural resources and public utilities.

Against this extenuation two answers may be adduced. Firstly, the legal position of the contracting parties must be so determined as to assure equal reciprocity. This consideration, obviously, is wholly independent of the capacity or incapacity of the parties to make use of their rights under the arrangement. What is essential is, should either be minded enough to exercise its rights, no restrictions other than those equally and reciprocally imposed, should prevent it. Secondly, while indeed admitting the present inability of the Filipinos to take advantage of parity in American territory, the case is otherwise with respect to Americans in the Philippines. Their massive capital and superior technology will enable them to exploit and operate Philippine natural resources and public utilities to a degree Filipinos themselves cannot hope to do.

From the foregoing observations it is submitted that the provisions of the Laurel-Langley Agreement on the mutual exploitation and operation of natural resources and public utilities do not meet the requirements of a fair and equal reciprocity.

2. *Whether vested rights acquired during the regime of parity will survive the termination of parity on July 3, 1974.*

Until the advent of parity the exploitation of natural resources and the operation of public utilities were limited to Filipinos or to corporations or associations whose capital is at least 60% Filipino-owned (Article XIII, Section 1; Article XIV, Section 8, *Constitution*). The reason for this marked preference for Filipino capital is best revealed in the following analysis of the proceedings of the Constitutional Convention:

"At the time of the framing of the Philippine Constitution, Filipino capital had been known to be rather shy. Filipinos hesitated as a general rule to invest a considerable sum of their capital for the development, exploitation, and utilization of the natural resources of the country. They had not as yet been so used to corporate enterprises

167

as the people of the West. This general apathy, the delegates knew, would mean the retardation of the development of the natural resources, unless foreign capital would be encouraged to come in and help in that development. They knew that the nationalization of the natural resources would certainly not encourage the investment of foreign capital into them. But *there was a general feeling in the Convention that it was better to have such a development retarded or even postponed altogether until such time when the Filipinos would be ready and willing to undertake it rather than permit the natural resources to be placed under the ownership or control of foreigners in order that they might be immediately developed, with the Filipinos of the future serving not as owners but at most as tenants or workers under foreign masters. By all means, the delegates believed, the natural resources should be conserved for Filipino posterity."* (Jose M. Aruego, *The Framing of the Philippine Constitution*, 1949, vol. 2, page 605.)

This nationalistic sentiment, which crystallized in specific constitutional provisions, was later approved by the President of the United States along with the rest of the Constitution on March 23, 1935. Eleven years later, when the Philippines lay prostrate and war-torn, the United States government laid it down as a condition for rehabilitation that the Philippine Constitution be amended in order to offer American citizens equal rights with Filipinos in the exploitation of natural resources and the operation of public utilities. Now known as parity, this grant of equal rights is embodied in the Ordinance appended to the Constitution. As earlier stated, exactly the same provisions found in the Ordinance were imported into the terms of the Laurel-Langley Agreement of 1956, except that the one-sided parity arrangement which prevailed under the U.S.-Philippine Executive Agreement of 1964 was modified to afford mutuality. How much reciprocity there is in this revised arrangement has already been discussed.

What remains now is to notice the crucial question of vested rights connected with the operation as well as termination of constitutional parity in our jurisdiction.

The parity Ordinance specifically states that equal rights enjoyed by the Americans in connection with the exploitation of natural resources and the operation of public utilities shall "in no case extend beyond the third of July nineteen hundred and seventy-four." With constitutional parity having ten more years to run it is not altogether unlikely for American citizens (more accurately: American corporations, pursuant to paragraph 2, Article VI of the Laurel-Langley Agreement) to apply for and secure the privileges vouchsafed to them. In every case such privileges are secured between now and July 3, 1974; for under the Constitution no license, concession or lease for the exploitation of natural resources shall be granted for a period longer than 25 years, renewable for another 25 years (Article XIII, Section 1) nor shall any franchise or certificate for the operation of public utilities be granted for a period exceeding 50 years (Article XIV, Section 8).

Under the provisions of the U.S.-Philippine Executive Agreement of 1946 and the parity Ordinance, the total number of years assigned for the enjoyment of parity by American citizens is 28 years, i.e., from 1946 to 1974. On this basis it is clear that any franchise or certificate secured by Americans for the operation of public utilities will necessarily outrun the termination date of parity and any license, lease or concession for the exploitation of natural resources should have been secured, at the latest, on or before 1949 in order to keep within the termination date.

In the light of these premises the question that naturally suggests itself is this. Does the termination of parity by July 3, 1974 involve the termination of rights, i.e., leases, concessions, licenses, certificates and franchises, gained under and by virtue of parity? If all these should continue beyond July 3, 1974, then their American holders may continue to enjoy their privileges exactly as Filipinos would, subject only to the termination of the period fixed by the Constitution for the enjoyment of such privileges. On the other hand, should these cease by July 3, 1974, then it would become necessary for their American holders either to reorganize in order to comply with the minority side of the 60%-40% capitalization required by the Constitution or, should they find this unpalatable, dismantle operations altogether.

It may be alleged, however, that these unpleasant consequences are not imperatively dictated by the termination of parity on July 3, 1974; that the termination cannot retrospectively operate to prejudice rights already acquired and that, this being the case, its only effect is to prevent fresh American enterprise from further enjoying parity from and after July 3, 1974. This latter point is rather obvious, if not platitudinous. From the express terms of both the parity Ordinance and Article XI, paragraph 1 of the Laurel-Langley Agreement the special privileges accorded to Americans will cease on July 3, 1974. The real issue is whether rights acquired *during the regime of parity* will survive the termination.

In support of the theory that these right will survive, the doctrine of vested rights is invoked. Philippine and American authorities define the right as follows:

> "Rights are vested when the right to enjoyment, present or prospective, has become the property of some particular person or persons as a particular interest." (*Balboa v. Farrales,* 51 Phil., 498, 502.)

> "A right is vested when its enjoyment, present or prospective, has become the property of a particular person as a present interest." (*Arnold & M. Co. v. Industrial Commission,* 40 ALR 1470, 1473.)

> "To be vested, in its accurate legal sense, a right must be complete and consummated, and of which the person to whom it belongs cannot be divested without his consent." (*Merchants' Bank v. Garrard,* 124 SE 715, 717.)

"It is defined as 'an immediate fixed right to present or future enjoyment' and 'an immediate fixed right of present enjoyment, or a present fixed right of future enjoyment'. Rights are said to be 'vested' when there is an ascertained person with a present right to present or future enjoyment; it is 'expectant' when it depends on the continuation of existing circumstances, such as the right of an heir to inherit, provided he survives the ancestor and the ancestor dies seised and intestate; and finally, is 'contingent' when it depends on the performance of some condition of the happening of some event before some other event or condition happens or is performed." (*11 Am. Jur.*, Section 370. Vested Right, page 1199.)

Based on the foregoing, it may be conceded that rights acquired by Americans under the regime of parity have indeed become vested. This, however, does not completely settle the question of their survival. To invoke the doctrine of vested rights purely and simply, without due regard to the termination of parity, is to over simplify, if not falsify, what in the original instance was a complex affair. For, originally, if parity was the source and the occasion for the grant of equal rights to Americans, so also was it the source and the occasion of the limitation of such enjoyment. In other words one can no more ignore vested right when considering the termination of parity any more than one can ignore its termination when considering vested rights. The task, therefore, is to examine both together and determine which, upon a balance of constitutional consideration, should prevail.

The grant of equal rights to Americans to exploit Philippine natural resources and operate public utilities finds its source in the Ordinance appended to the Constitution. Said Ordinance provides:

"Notwithstanding the provisions of section one, Article Thirteen, section eight, Article Fourteen, of the foregoing Constitution, during the ef-

171

fectivity of the Executive Agreement entered into by the President of the Philippines with the President of the United States on the fourth of July, nineteen hundred and forty-six, pursuant to the provisions of Commonwealth Act Numbered Seven hundred and thirty-three, but in no case to extend beyond the third of July, nineteen hundred and seventy-four, the disposition, exploitation, development, and utilization of all agricultural, timber, and mineral lands of the public domain, waters, minerals, coal, petroleum and other mineral oils, all forces and sources of potential energy, and other natural resources of the Philippines, and the operation of public utilities, shall, if open to any person, be open to citizens of the United States and to all forms of business enterprise owned or controlled, directly or indirectly, by citizens of the United States in the same manner as to, and under the same conditions, imposed upon, citizens of the Philippines or corporations or associations owned or controlled by citizens of the Philippines."

Since the foregoing provision sufficiently states the rule by means of which Americans may exercise the rights extended to them and, further, contains no indication, either express or implied, requiring legislative intervention in order to make effective such enjoyment, the presumption may be indulged that it is self-executing. In terms of its practical operation this means that, upon the approval of the Ordinance as part of the Constitution, Americans automatically acquired the rights hitherto conferred exclusively upon Filipino citizens by Article XIII, Section I and Article XIV, Section 8 of the Constitution. As negative proof that the Ordinance has always been treated as self-executing, the observation may here be cited that the Congress has never found it necessary to implement it.

Considering the cardinal importance of the rule on self-executing provisions, the statement of the rule had better be given:

172

"One of the recognized rules is that a constitutional provision is not self-executing when it merely lays down general principles, but that it is self-executing if it supplies the sufficient rule by means of which the right which it grants may be enjoyed and protected, or the duty which it imposes may be enforced without the aid of legislative enactment." (6 RCL, Section 55 page 59.)

Reverting to the Ordinance, it will be noticed that if the clause which grants equal rights to Americans is self-executing, the clause which limits the enjoyment of such right, viz, " . . . in no case to extend beyond the third of July nineteen hundred and seventy-four", is likewise self-executing. Speaking of the termination date, this means that, again, independently of any intervening act of Congress, constitutional parity shall automatically cease on July 3, 1974.

Since the termination of parity by July 3, 1974 will *automatically* restore the exclusiveness of Article XIII, Section 1 and Article XIV, Section 8 in favor of Filipino citizens, it would follow that the termination date set in the Ordinance is more than merely a termination date. It would logically constitute a prohibition upon further continuance of parity, pursuant to the established canon of interpretation that —

"Prohibitory provisions in a constitution are usually self-executory to the extent that anything done in violation of them is void." (6 RCL, Section 58, page 62.)

This, then, is the meaning of the clause in the Ordinance, viz, "in no case to extend beyond the third of July nineteen hundred seventy-four", that it does not merely terminate parity but that it also prohibits it. And *the prohibition resides in the automatic revival of the exclusiveness guaranteed to Filipino citizens by article XIII, Section 1 and Article XIV, Section 8. Being exclusive in character, these provisions would automatically and necessarily pro-*

173

hibit non-Filipinos from further enjoying the privileges gained thereunder.

It will of course be urged contrarily that the prohibition is prospective; that it is intended to prohibit parity from and after July 3, 1974; and that rights already acquired during the regime of parity, having become vested, must be respected until their periods, foreseeably going beyond July 3, 1974, have run out.

That these rights have become vested for the period of time during parity subsists is readily acknowledged, but that they should continue to maintain their vested character beyond July 3, 1974 is untenable, constitutionally and from the contemporaneous circumstances which gave rise to them.

First, from the constitutional angle. It has already been shown that upon the termination of parity on July 3, 1974, the exclusive privileges contained in Article XIII, Section 1 and Article XIV, Section 8 are automatically restored to Filipino citizen. Allowing for the contention that American privileges will continue to subsist beyond July 3, 1974, a situation will arise where Article XIII, Section I and Article XIV, Section 8 will, *at one and the same time, be both exclusive and non-exclusive,* that is, exclusive for Filipino citizens and non-exclusive in the sense of admitting aliens (i.e., Americans). Assuming now, and not improbably, that a Filipino citizen seeks to enjoin Americans from further exercising their parity privileges, the relief he seeks is confronted by a constitutional paradox. On the one hand, his constitutional right to have Americans excluded is clear; on the other, it is rendered inoperative and ineffectual by alien rights that are claimed to be founded on the Constitution.

In the face of this paradox the executive and judicial branches of the Government may either choose to grant the relief or deny it. If they grant it, that simply would mean that American parity privileges have no vested character beyond July 3, 1974. If they deny it, then it would mean that *the executive and judicial organs of the Gov-*

174

ernment shall have been rendered impotent to enforce the provisions of Article XIII, Section 1 and Article XIV, Section 8 which, from and after July 3, 1974, have automatically revived in favor of Filipinos the exclusiveness of privileges therein provided. But if this is so, then the fault would lie less with the inability of the Government to give due course to the relief than to the Executive Agreement of 1946, later renewed in the Laurel-Langley Agreement of 1956, which created the inability. It is this inability which, should the theory of vested rights beyond 1974 prevail, will ultimately involve the Government in a constitutional *impassé.*

The question now is, should the parity provision of the Executive Agreement of 1946 (as restated in the Ordinance appended to the Constitution and renewed in the Laurel-Langley Agreement of 1956) be so construed as to impair the powers of the Government to enforce the exclusiveness in favor of Filipinos of Article XIII, Section 1 and Article XIV, Section 8 of the Constitution upon the termination of parity on July 3, 1974? Corwin, a respected authority on constitutional law, says:

> " . . . a treaty to which the United States is party is not only an international compact but also 'law of the land' in which latter respect *it may not override the Constitution.* Therefore, it may not change the character of the government which is established by the Constitution *nor require an organ of that government to relinquish its constitutional powers."* (Edward S. Corwin, *The Constitution and What It Means Today,* 12th ed., page 109, Princeton University Press: 1958.) Italic Supplied.

As in the United States, so also in the Philippines a treaty may not override the Constitution. This is unmistakably clear from Article VIII, Section 2, Clause 1 of the Constitution which vests in the Supreme Court appellate jurisdiction over cases where the constitutionality of any treaty is in issue: The words of Corwin, therefore, have special relevance to the question on hand. Of greater authority but with same degree of relevance is the following pronouncement of the United States Supreme Court.

"The treaty power, as expressed in the Constitution, in terms unlimited except by those restraints which are found in that instrument against the action of its government or of its departments, are those arising from the nature of the government itself and of that of the States. *It would not be contended that it extends so far as to authorize what the constitution* forbids, or a change in character of the government or in that of one of the States, or a cession of any territory of the latter without its consent." (Geofroy v. Riggs, 133 U.S. 258, 267; 33 L ed., 2d. 644, 654.) Italic Supplied.

While, indeed, the parity agreement with the United States must receive a liberal interpretation in order to effect the purpose for which it was entered into, such liberal interpretation does not warrant the survival of vested rights beyond July 3, 1974, *else that would require the Government to relinquish its constitutional powers of safeguarding the exclusiveness of Article XIII, Section 1 and Article XIV, Section 8 in favor of Filipino citizens from and after July 3, 1974. To contend otherwise would be to support alien vested rights at the expense of the Constitution.*

At this juncture a question of administrative significance may be interposed. Is the Philippine Government bound to respect licenses, consessions, leases or certificates issued by administrative agencies to American applicants for periods running beyond July 3, 1974? On the principle herein argued that vested rights corresponding to these licenses, concessions, leases or certificates cannot last beyond July 3, 1974, it would follow that no vested right can arise from the administrative interpretations of parity that these licenses, concessions, leases or certificates can enjoy their vested character beyond July 3, 1974. As the Philippine Supreme Court very pithily said:

"A vested right cannot spring from a wrong interpretation (of the law). This is too clear to require elaboration. x x x "It seems too clear for serious argument that an administrative officer cannot change a law enacted by Congress. A regulation is merely an interpretation of the statute when once determined to have been erroneous becomes a nullity (Ben Stocher *et al.*, 12 B.T.A. 1351)." (*Emilio Hilado v. Collector of Internal Revenue*, 53 O.G. 2481 [1956])

On the basis of this ruling administrative agencies which have honestly and erroneously, authorized leases, licenses, concessions, or certificates for periods beyond the expiration date of parity may either reverse themselves or be reversed by superior authority.

From a consideration of the contemporaneous circumstances which gave rise to the vested rights, it may likewise be exhibited that the vested character of those rights cannot survive the termination date of parity. Examination of the parity Ordinance leaves no room for doubt that contemporaneously with the grant of special privileges to the Americans was the imposition of the time-limit. This time-limit, therefore, is deemed written into whatever privileges American citizens may acquire under the Ordinance. Hence, it cannot be raised as a valid objection that the extinction of vested rights by 1974 would constitute an undue retrospective operation.

FOR ALL THE FOREGOING, it is respectfully submitted that vested rights acquired under the regime of parity will not survive the termination date of the parity Ordinance.

APPENDIX

NATIONAL ECONOMIC COUNCIL
RESOLUTION NO. 90 (65)*

WHEREAS, the constitution of the Philippines provides, as follows:

"SECTION 1 *(Article XIII).* All agricultural, timber, and mineral lands of the public domain, waters, minerals, coal, petroleum, and other mineral oils, all forces of potential energy, and other natural resources of the Philippines belong to the State, and their disposition, exploitation, development, or utilization shall be limited to citizens of the Philippines, or to corporations or associations at least sixty per centum of the capital of which is owned by such citizens, subject to any existing right, grant, lease or concession at the time of the inauguration of the Government established under this Constitution. Natural resources, with the exception of public agricultural land, shall not be alienated, and no license, concession, or lease for the exploitation, development, or utilization of any of the natural resources shall be granted for a period exceeding twenty-five years, renewable for another twenty-five years, except as to water rights for irrigation, water supply, fisheries, or industrial uses other than the development of water power, in which cases beneficial use may be the measure and the limit of the grant."

"SECTION 8 *(Article XIV).* No franchise, certificate, or any other form of authorization for the operation of a public utility shall be granted except to citizens of the Philippines or to corporations or other entities organized under the laws of the Philippines, sixty per centum of the capital

---

* NEC Resolution No. 90 (65) was passed by the National Economic Council on the basis of Chairman Hilarion M. Henares, Jr.'s report on "The Termination of Constitutional Parity and Vested Rights" This resolution is the first to be passed unanimously by the council in its history.

of which is owned by citizens of the Philippines, nor shall such franchise, certificate, or authorization be exclusive in character or for a longer period than fifty years. No franchise or right shall be granted to any individual, firm, or corporation, except under the condition that it shall be subject to amendment, alteration, or repeal by the Congress when the public interest so requires."

WHEREAS, the Ordinance Appended to the Constitution provides, as follows:

"Notwithstanding the provisions of section one, Article Thirteen, and section eight, Article Fourteen, of the foregoing Constitution, during the effectivity of the Executive Agreement entered into by the President of the Philippines with the President of the United States on the fourth of July, nineteen hundred and forty-six, pursuant to the provisions of Commonwealth Act Number Seven hundred and thirty-three, but in no case to extend beyond the third of July, nineteen hundred and seventy-four, the disposition, exploitation, development, and utilization of all agricultural, timbers, and mineral lands of the public domain, waters, minerals, coal, petroleum, and other mineral oils, all forces of potential energy, and other natural resources of the Philippines, and the operation of public utilities, shall, if open to any person, be open to citizens of the United States and to all forms of business enterprise owned or controlled, directly or indirectly, by citizens of the United States in the same manner as to, and under the same conditions imposed upon, citizens of the Philippines or corporations or associations owned or controlled by citizens of the Philippines."

WHEREAS, it has come to the knowledge of the National Economic Council that some agencies of the Government of the Philippines, in the exercise of their administrative functions, may have overlooked the above-quoted provisions of the Constitution;

NOW, THEREFORE, IN THE NATIONAL INTEREST, BE IT RESOLVED, AS IT IS HEREBY RESOLVED, BY THE NATIONAL ECONOMIC COUNCIL:

179

To state and announce the Council's position, as follows:

First, that it would be advisable for all Government Agencies in the exercise of their administrative functions, to limit up to (not beyond) July 3, 1974, the period of all new contracts, licenses, concessions, leases, certificates and other forms of authorization, granted to citizens of the United States and to all forms of business enterprise owned or controlled directly or indirectly by citizens of the United States, for "the disposition, exploitation, development or utilization of agricultural, timber and mineral lands of the public domain, waters, minerals, coal, petroleum, and other mineral oils, all forces of potential energy, and other natural resources of the Philippines," as well as "the operation of public utilities";

Second, that it would likewise be advisable for all Government Agencies to examine or reexamine all old and existing contracts, licenses, concessions, leases, certificates and other forms of authorization, to determine which of them, if any, are violative of the Constitutional provisions aforesaid, and, in the interest of fairness and to avoid possible misunderstanding, to take immediate steps to inform all concerned that after July 3, 1974, the rights so granted shall cease, subject, however, to possible renewal or extension if and when the citizenship requirements prescribed in the Constitution shall have been complied with.

APPROVED, February 18, 1965.

(Sgd.) Ramon M. Durano, *Congressman*
(Sgd.) C. Balmaceda, *Sec. of Commerce & Industry*
(Sgd.) Ramon Bagatsing, *Congressman*
(Sgd.) Andres V. Castillo, *Governor, Central Bank*
(Sgd.) Pablo Lorenzo, *Chairman, DBP*
(Sgd.) Augusto Cesar Espiritu, *Private Sector*
(Sgd.) Lorenzo Tañada, *Senator*
(Sgd.) Eugenio Padua, *Private Sector*
(Sgd.) Rogaciano M. Mercado, *Congressman*
(Sgd.) Gil J. Puyat, *Senator*
(Sgd.) Ambrosio Padilla, *Senator*
(Sgd.) Cipriano Cid, *Private Sector*
(Sgd.) Hilarion M. Henares, Jr., *Chairman, NEC*

Appendix X

About the Author

Hilarion M. Henares, Jr. is the bridge of the last generation of nationalist writers and the coming one. His passionate nationalist ideology which is not different from that of the legendary intellectual. Senator Recto, is present in his more important writings and public pronouncements.

His probings on the present stirrings in our kind of society deserves more than a passing notice.

But Larry Henares is more than a spokesman of nationalist economic philosophy. He is also a lover of the good life. His interests in arts and letters is deep-rooted. He admires Adlai Stevenson for his nobility and for his intellectual pride.

In some extent, Recto and Stevenson are the models that he seemed to adopt in his public life. His capacity for oral communication more than confirm this attitude.

Henares had been, among all others, head of a multi-million peso industrial complex and President of the Philippine Chamber of Industries. During the Macapagal regime, he was the highest paid member of the cabinet as Chairman of the National Economic Council. He had also an occasion to be a Dean of a university at a very young age of twenty-five.

On May 15, 1965, Henares, Jr. was conferred a degree of Doctor of Economics, honoris causa, by the Arancta University "for outstanding contribution to the national welfare as an educator, entrepreneur, writer, civic leader, economist, devoted public servant, and a nationalist."

Clearly young as he is, Henares is at the pinnacle of his career. The triangulation of events will in the end inexorably point to his passionate destiny as a leader.

As NEC Chairman, Secretary Henares took the initiative to conduct the now famous hearings on the Laurel-

Langley Agreement in 1964 — a development that that crystallized public opinion on the "parity rights" granted to American citizens, provoked a series of public demonstrations against the American Embassy, and set the stage for a resurgence of nationalist fervor, culminating in a national consensus not to extend parity rights to Americans beyond 1974, the terminal date of the treaty! Even the U.S. State Department was constrained to declare that the American government shall not seek such extension.

Henares went further. Through his initiative, the Council passed a resolution declaring it against national interest to recognize the "vested" rights of Americans" now enjoying parity to continue enjoying it beyond 1974.

Several policy resolutions passed by the Council during Secretary Henares' tenure reflect the nationalist influence which he injected into the administration of President Macapagal.

One of these, in unequivocal terms, condemned the practice and existence of wholly-owned subsidiaries in the Philippines, and declared it a national policy to extend investment incentives only to joint ventures and wholly owned Filipino enterprises.

Another, condemned the attempts of foreign lobbyists to emasculate the Retail Trade Nationalization Act. And another opposed in principle the entry of foreign investments in an area already pre-empted by Filipino pioneers sufficiently producing for the domestic market.

Appendix Y

What they said

One of the most brilliant in my cabinet . . Secretary Henares has a sharp intellect and a mighty pen. These and his knowledge of economics and healthy nationalism make him one of the truly valuably leaders of our people today.

DIOSDADO MACAPAGAL
President of the Republic of the Philippines

Henares' writings clearly indicate the tone and magnitude of his basic philosophy and ideas. Whether it be in economics, or in his more intense moments, in matters affecting the dilemma of man himself in this mechanized world, Henares displays a passion for truth and an intelligence capable of assimilating seemingly disparate aspects of culture and presenting them in the coherence of a solid logical structure.

CARLOS P. ROMULO
President, University of the Philippines
ex-President, United Nations Assembly

Let me tell you about Hilarion Henares, Jr., the young president of the Philippine Chamber of Industries . . . Why do I tell you all this? Because you might see in Mr. Henares, in the men and women of such a movement and in the spirit they would excite in the people, the image of America — individual initiative, a forward progressive attitude . . .

SENATOR RAUL S. MANGLAFUS
in a speech before the Asian-Amencan Assembly,
Kuala Lumpur, 10 April 1963

The youthful chairman of the National Economic Council has always been sensitive to encroachments on the rights and dignities of the Filipino people . . . Chairman Henares told a high American official that he was meddling in Philippine affairs, practically threw him out of his office, and then filed a protest through the department of foreign affairs, against the American official's presumptuous behaviour.

J. V. Cruz
Columnist of the Manila Times

Appendix Z

Why I Publish and/or Reprint Books
And Why Free
By Tatay Jobo Elizes, Self-Publisher

Writings are timeless and they act as mirrors of history. They remain relevant anytime. I have seen a lot of good writings in the internet, in magazines and newspapers. But most writers have only one or two articles and therefore not enough material to be published as a book. And yet, many of them need to be published. So the idea of collecting all these various writings hit me. I myself cannot come up with enough material. I decided to offer my services to publish anybody's worth-while writings in one fairly good sized book, in paperback or pocketbook form. Their ability to publish is solved in a nutshell.

There are also writers who write a lot but never publish them. There are also old books with no more prints available. The solution is to publish/reprint.

I am offering these services free of charge because of the availability of print-books-on- demand (POD) system nowadays. I can produce the book, but the prints are not free.

Why put your writings in a book? And not just in the internet? The book will always be there among your collections or libraries. Not all use the internet. The internet access has its technical problems.

For those looking for a publisher, especially if you have a novel or many essays, I can produce the paperback book under your own authorship at no cost. I can produce art books, family tree books, family albums/pictorials, biographies, joke books, songhits books, travelogues, reunions, color or black & white, etc.

Please buy online as paperback or kindle at **http:// tinyurl.com/mj76ccq** (copy and paste to your browser).

oo0Ooo

www.ingramcontent.com/pod-product-compliance
Lightning Source LLC
Chambersburg PA
CBHW062158280526
45788CB00001B/357